The Realist Bride b

First Edition

Table of Contents

INTRODUCTION

Hey, I'm Jessica. I'm a newlywed, so it's fresh in my mind how incredibly overwhelming the entire wedding planning process can be.

When I was engaged, I wished for a tell-all how-to guide like this. It's normal to feel stressed out, overwhelmed and frustrated with planning, and I wrote this book to help you get through it all. I'll explain in great detail each phase of the planning process (in the order that you need to do it!), and I'll also tell you what the wedding industry won't, and I'm not going to sugarcoat it, because that's not my style. I'll help you through the good, the bad and the ugly, and I'll share some personal stories to prove to you that you really aren't alone in this. Don't worry: I'm going to tell you how to plan your wedding without losing your shit.

No stone is left unturned. From how much you should tip your vendors to when you should kick someone out of your bridal party to how to land the perfect wedding dress, we're gonna hit it all. I've also included tons of money saving tips throughout the chapters so you can have the wedding of your dreams without going into debt.

I got married to my husband Joey when I was 28 years old at a wedding that we paid for and I planned by myself. I'm going to tell you how I did it, and how you can do it too. Let's do this.

1:

GET ORGANIZED

Really. Do it. Organization is the key to planning your wedding. It'll be so much easier and you'll be way less stressed than someone who is all over the place. It's kind of like when you have a clean house versus a messy one; you feel calmer and more in control when everything is in place and overwhelmed when things aren't in order.

I have a few pieces of organizational advice.

First off, get a binder, tabs, and a three hole punch. I went to Target and bought the most beautiful binder they had. It makes it more fun and easier to stick to if the binder is jazzy. Use the tabs to separate sections. An example of some sections you should create:

Signed Contracts (everything you book should be in writing; I don't care if they're a family friend)

Spreadsheets (Budget, RSVPs, etc.)

Rehearsal Dinner Restaurant Options

Wedding Task Checklist

Wedding Day Timeline

...and so on, and so on.

If your documents are all in one place, not only do you stay organized, but you stay on task. Do I sound like

Monica Geller yet? It's because we are the same person.

Second, put together a document for every company category that you haven't booked yet. (Bridal Salons, Floral, Design, DJs, etc.) Look into at least four businesses per category and keep notes on conversations you have with people. If they're rude, toss 'em. If they don't care about a potential client, they sure as hell won't care once they get your deposit money. If they have negative reviews online, read what the reviews say; depending on what the problem was, whether or not the vendor responded, and the number of negative reviews, toss those too. There are SO many vendors in every city that it is impossible to talk to them all, so you have to have a process of weeding them out.

Third, choose wisely when selecting a Maid of Honor. Being friends with someone for a long time or feeling pressure to pick your sister does not mean that they are the best choice for you. Your MOH will be your right hand woman throughout your entire planning process. Trust me, you don't want to eff this one up. One of my bridesmaids got married last year and her MOH made her experience *much* harder instead of making it easier. Unless you want your bridal shower at Denny's and you want to add coordinating with all of your bridesmaids for every task to your already packed schedule, do yourself a favor and pick the best woman for the job. If she is truly your best friend, she will cater to your needs (unless you become a crazy bridezilla, in which case you can kiss any help at all goodbye.)

Finally: read this book. Don't let it sit on your tablet for months without reading every chapter. I am a straight shooter and I will tell you like it is, and I will help you get through the tough times. Stick with it, and go back to chapters later that you found extra helpful.

If you're close to your wedding and you are feeling overwhelmed with stuff to get done, it's not too late to get your shit together. Break it down by category and take your time.

2:

WHAT NO ONE TELLS YOU ABOUT BEING ENGAGED

This is probably not going to be the best time of your life the way magazines and television shows will lead you to believe. **It is hard to be a bride.** No one thinks to tell you that. I am here to tell you that while being engaged to the love of your life is exciting, and there are certainly magical moments (like finding your perfect dress!) that's about all the magic there is. People become crazy, people let you down, and everything is 1,000 times more expensive than you thought it would be.

When you first get engaged, people fawn over you asking all about it, but that eventually goes away and you're left to plan the largest event of your life, most of the time by yourself. Well, you're not alone, sister. I'm here to help.

Start Saving Money Before You're Engaged

One of the hard parts of planning a wedding is that life doesn't stop just because you're getting married. You still have your job, your everyday responsibilities and everyday payments to worry about on top of organizing a huge event.

If you're reading this, you're probably already engaged, but it's not too late to start saving. Make a list of what you spend your money on each month, and anything that's not an essential, cut it out or cut it down dramatically. It's only temporary and it makes life easier in the long run. My cat had to have an expensive emergency surgery a few months before my final payments were due. What I'm trying to tell you is the universe doesn't care that you're getting married; shit happens, and not all the money you have set aside is necessarily going to get you through it when you have a bunch of new wedding related payments to make.

Don't open up a bunch of credit cards to pay for the wedding. It's going to be tempting as the payments start to rack up, but the last thing you want to do is start off your new life together in debt. I love weddings as much as the next person, but it's not okay to put you and your fiancé under financial hardship just to have one. Instead, open a joint account that is strictly a wedding fund that you both contribute to weekly. If you don't think it's feasible in the near future to afford the wedding you want, have a longer engagement period. Your fiancé will probably appreciate your level-headedness.

Don't Make Everything About Your Wedding

I know that the most important thing going on right now is your wedding, but it can become an unhealthy obsession and stress you out like you wouldn't believe. This is where a hobby or project comes in.

For me, it was refinishing my kitchen cabinets. It's nice to have something non wedding related to focus your energy on, and some things even give you new topics of conversation that AREN'T ABOUT YOUR WEDDING! I hate to tell you this, but your friends and family (and probably your fiancé) are probably dying for you to give it a rest with the wedding convos. Take on a small and inexpensive home project, join a book club, take painting lessons...you can do something that works a part of your brain that you'd like to explore more, or you can do something mindless that doesn't take much involvement. Just be sure to get your mind off of your wedding a few hours a week. It'll lead to a healthier engagement period.

Communication is Key

My mom and I had a huge blowout of a fight a few months after I got engaged. The reason it got to be such a screamfest (okay, I was the only one screaming) was because prior to that day, instead of nipping things in the bud that were bothering me, I didn't say anything. I was attempting to keep the peace by keeping my mouth shut when she made comments I didn't agree with, and by the end of a string of these comments, I completely lost my shit and let everything come out at once. I am a very outspoken person so not speaking my mind from the get go was like poison to my brain. As soon as I let all of the toxic out, I felt relief, but I also felt sadness and guilt because of the scale of my reaction. Had I calmly stated my issues or put my foot down a little harder in prior conversations, I doubt it would have gotten to the point that it did.

It may sound crazy, especially if you're early on in your engagement, but things tend to build up with your fiancé too. There's a lot of strain on your relationship because you're dealing with things you haven't dealt with before, and the politics and cost of wedding planning don't exactly help your situation. If you aren't on the same page about something with the wedding, such as who you're inviting, what kind of wedding you want to have and *especially* the budget, it's going to cause a crack that'll turn into a full on fracture in your relationship if you don't address it and figure out a solution right away.

Don't let resentment build; it will only make things worse. If you're having an issue with someone, I encourage you to think about what is bothering you and why, and tactfully discuss it with the person that it applies to, whether it's a family member or a bridesmaid. Address the situation head on (not in text or email!) Go to lunch and figure it out. It's likely that they've been feeling your energy and so it may not even come as a surprise. Who knows, maybe they have a bone to pick too. Get it all out and then move on. Stress causes outbursts, and it also causes wrinkles… and *nobody* needs wrinkles.

A List of Acronyms

Online wedding forums are a source of community among brides, and boy, do they LOVE acronyms on wedding boards. You'll probably end up visiting a board or two during your engagement, and you'll need this guide to figure out what the hell everyone is trying to say.

FH: Future Husband
SO: Significant Other
MOH: Maid of Honor
BM: Best Man or Bridesmaid (Can't we figure out a different one for them?)
MOB: Mother of the Bride
FOB: Father of the Bride
MOG: Mother of the Groom
FOG: Father of the Groom

ILs: In-laws (if anything ending in IL is prefaced with an F, it stands for Future)
SIL: Sister-in-law
BIL: Brother-in-law
MIL: Mother-in-law
FIL: Father-in-law
LDR: Long Distance Relationship
AHR: At Home Reception
DW: Destination Wedding
FG: Flower Girl
RB: Ring Bearer
JP: Justice of the Peace
MUA: Makeup Artist
OOTG: Out of Town Guests
LTBM: Living Together Before Marriage
STD: Save-the-Date (...really? Just spell this one out.)

The Wedding Industry

As vulnerable brides, we are all being manipulated to conform to what the wedding industry and society tell us are the things we *need* in order to throw a great wedding, even if we don't realize it.

As soon as you mention the word "wedding" people within the industry begin to salivate because they can jack up the price of whatever they're selling. One of my bridesmaids and I went to a couple bridal salons looking for a dress for her daughter, who was my flower girl. She was a year and a half old at the time of our wedding and it was almost impossible to find a dress her size. (I didn't realize that flower girl dresses can take 3 months to come in after being ordered or else I would have just gone on Etsy.) The flower girl dress ended up being more expensive than the bridesmaid dresses. When I told Joey about the price he didn't flinch, and instead said "Yeah, because how many times are you going to order a flower girl dress? They need to get as much money out of you as they can."

There are some things that whether society cares or not I think are a "must", such as an open bar (making people pay for drinks is rude. My parents went to a wedding that had a cash bar and people were so mad they started opening their wedding cards and taking money out of them). However, as I planned my wedding I found myself thinking about what people were going to think and say about our wedding. But really...who cares? It should be about you and your significant other and it should be exactly how you want it. You want to serve pizza for dinner? Go for it. You want to buy your dress from a department store? Cool. You're getting married at your house? That's awesome. What we're told we have to do by advertisements and TV shows aren't law. While we are all affected somewhat by family, friend and societal expectations, especially when parents are contributing to the problem, it's important not to lose sight of what it is you really want. In the years to come the only people who will be thinking about your wedding day are you and your spouse, and you want to be sure it was exactly how you wanted it to be.

The Pinterest Bride

Speaking of expectations, let's talk about Pinterest. I was pleasantly surprised at the direction it provided me while planning my wedding, but it can be a slippery slope.

If you've been living under a rock and don't know what Pinterest is, it's a social media site where you can search for things like recipes, workouts, and wedding inspiration, and if you see something you like, you "pin" it to your online board to add to your collection. It's basically a Dream Board with links. Pinterest hasn't been around for long so brides today are lucky to have this resource to go to for collective creative brainstorming.

FOR THE LOVE OF GOD, PLEASE DELETE THE MESSAGE FROM THE PINNER BEFORE YOU. When you are pinning an item, the message from the last person who pinned the image remains there until you delete it or write your own. Use the message box to write the reason for pinning the photo or to write a little note to yourself about it.

When I first signed up and looked for wedding related images, my searches were very general, so I wasn't getting the kind of results that I wanted. If you just search "wedding" you're going to get all different kinds of wedding related items that are probably not what you are really searching for. Be as specific with your keywords as possible. Once I started searching for things like "black and white wedding" or "white floral centerpieces" I got more images that helped me put together an idea of what I wanted my wedding to look like.

Another way I used Pinterest was for my bridal shower. I made my bridal shower board available to be pinned on from my bridesmaids. They could see examples of what I liked, and when they pinned something that wasn't my style, I just deleted the pin or left notes in the box that went with the picture. This is how my MOH and I decided on my shower invitations and I think it makes it a little easier on everyone to have a clear vision of each others' ideas (especially for bridesmaids who live far away). However, some things that we liked weren't always feasible.

Enter: The Pinterest Bride. These are the women who obsess over Pinterest photos of beautiful yet unattainable weddings. Although I found Pinterest to be very helpful for putting together ideas, especially for someone who is not especially creative such as myself, I also noticed that they are professional photos and most of them are taken at hundred thousand dollar, and even million dollar, events. This raises expectations for the everyday bride, and when their wedding inevitably doesn't look as grandiose as the photos on Pinterest, they'll be grossly disappointed.

Additionally, because so many people are pinning photos of "Do It Yourself" decorations that look amazing and are no doubt a bitch to put together, this is going to put some serious pressure on brides who are having a mostly DIY wedding. I tend to think DIY brides are a little nuts…there is enough to do already when planning a wedding without individually putting together every piece of it. Please consider that most of those super cute DIY items you're seeing have not been prepared by the bride but by an event coordinator who pays a vendor or member of their staff to do it.

Pinterest has been a great tool for those planning a wedding to gain inspiration, but being inspired does not mean that your event needs to look exactly like the one in the photo. Remember to keep your expectations realistic. Think about what exactly it is that you like about the photos you've pinned and then share them with your floral or event designer and let them take care of the details. It's their job to make your vision come to life within your budget, and having photos to see what your style looks like will help them bring your event together perfectly.

3:

CREATING A BUDGET

The most important thing you can do for yourself and your fiancé is to come up with a realistic budget. This way you won't set yourself up for failure and you can decide how much to set aside for each part of the wedding day.

Prioritize which areas mean the most to you. If you go over budget on an important item (and you will go over budget somewhere), you can take the budget down in another area that isn't as important to you.

Wedding budgets range from $1,000 to upwards of $100,000. There's nothing wrong with any wedding budget, as long as you can afford it and it doesn't put anyone in a financial conundrum.

Who Pays For What?

It's not quite like it was in years past when the bride's family paid for everything. (What kind of bullshit rule is that, anyway?) Now more than ever we are seeing both sets of parents going halvsies with each other on the wedding, or together they'll pay for half and the bride and groom pay for half, or, more often than people think, the parents don't contribute at all.

Nobody likes talking about money, but there's no getting around it when it comes to a wedding, and the earlier you do it, the better position you'll be in for planning purposes. You'll want to talk to both sets of parents and ask what, if anything, they plan on contributing. Some people will give a number, and some people will say "I'll pay for the dress" or "I'll pay for the reception." Make sure you get specifics, though, because they might think a dress costs $500 and you think a dress costs $5,000. And that goes for anything, from the reception dinner to the honeymoon.

Basically, no one is required to pay for your wedding, so be gracious about any contribution or lack thereof.

As far as you and your fiancé go: whatever is left for you to pay for, you need to both be on the same page about how much you're willing to put toward the wedding. Overspending or making a large financial decision without discussing it first will lead to resentment, and that's no way to start your new life together.

Things people forget In their budget: tax and tips. People don't work them into their budgets and it can make a pretty huge difference. Dependent on your contract, you're going to have to pay some service charges (gratuity) and tax on dinner and drinks. You're also going to have to pay tax on your dress, your flowers, and most every other thing on your list.

Who Gets Tipped, and How Much?

When creating a budget, always allow for gratuity. Check every contract you sign and see if any tip is included. For those that aren't, give sealed envelopes with the cash and write on the envelope who they go to and have your wedding coordinator or trusted member of your family distribute the envelopes to the right people.

Hair & Makeup Artist: 20%

Catering Manager: Only applicable if you're having food catered from outside of your venue. Check the contract, but if it doesn't include gratuity, tip anywhere from $250-$500.

Wedding musicians: $15-$25 per musician.

Limo Driver: 15-20%. (Check your contract; gratuity may already be included.)

Delivery Staff: Most of your vendors will require delivery, including your florist, your cake bakery, linen rental company, etc. $5-$10 per person is the standard for delivery gratuity.

Reception Staff: Check your contract, because gratuity is likely paid directly to the venue for wait staff. If not, plan on tipping 15-20% of the pre-tax food bill.

Bartenders: Some bartenders leave a tip jar out, but for those that don't or are prohibited to do so by your venue, tip 15% of the bar charge.

Reception Attendants: If your venue has coat check and/or bathroom attendants, they should be tipped $1 per guest.

Optional Tips

Event Planner/Coordinator: Though this one is optional, if your coordinator has done a nice job, you should get them something. A gift, such as a flower arrangement, gift card to a spa, or something more personal is a nice gesture.

Officiant: If you're getting married at a church, you'll likely be asked to make a donation of at least $100. If you're having a non-denominational ceremony, you can offer an optional tip of $50.

Photographer and Videographer: If your photographer and videographer are owners of the business, do not tip them. If they bring assistants, though, you can tip them $50-$100.

DJ: Again, totally optional, but if they did a great job and you want to show your appreciation, tip $50.

Florist: No tip required, but my florist was so fantastic and helpful to me that I gave him a gift. I encourage you to do the same for any vendor who went out of their way for you.

The average wedding in the United States costs over $25,000 (excluding the engagement ring and honeymoon). Here's a sample budget spreadsheet for wedding costs based on a $25,000 budget. The **Estimated Cost** column is what you should use when initially creating your budget. As you start to sign contracts and purchase items, update the budget in the **Actual Cost** column. This can keep you in check when you've started spending more than you thought you would in certain areas so you can try to bring the budget down in other areas. Keep track of deposits you've put down in the **Paid** column, and put the balance of what you owe in the **Due** column.

	A	B	C		D	E	F
1		Estimated Cost	Actual Cost		Paid	Due	
2	Floral/décor	$2,500.00		$2,700.00	$1,000.00	$1,700.00	
3	Rentals: Chairs/Linens/Covers	$400.00		$600.00	$300.00	$300.00	
4	Photography	$2,500.00		$3,000.00	$1,500.00	$1,500.00	
5	DJ, uplighting	$1,200.00		$1,400.00	$400.00	$1,000.00	
6	Cake, cake stand, serving set	$300.00		$500.00	$250.00	$250.00	
7	Food, beverage, tax, gratuity	$8,000.00		$9,500.00	$5,000.00	$4,500.00	
8	Ceremony Musicians plus tip	$150.00		$150.00	$150.00	$0.00	
9	Invitations	$600.00		$800.00	$800.00	$0.00	
10	Save the Dates	$125.00		$125.00	$125.00	$0.00	
11	Postage	$150.00		$180.00	$180.00	$0.00	
12	Officiant	$300.00		$300.00	$300.00	$0.00	
13	Ceremony Room Rental Fee	$500.00		$500.00	$500.00	$0.00	
14	Ring Bearer Pillow/Flower Girl Basket	$50.00		$50.00	$50.00	$0.00	
15	Tuxedo		$150.00	Free with groomsmen rentals	$0.00	$0.00	
16	Rings	$1,000.00		$900.00	$900.00	$0.00	
17	Dress	$2,500.00		$2,800.00	$1,680.00	$1,120.00	
18	Favors	$500.00		$600.00	$600.00	$0.00	
19	Bridal Hair & Makeup plus tip	$350.00		$375.00	$0.00	$375.00	
20	Videographer	$500.00		$800.00	$400.00	$400.00	
21	Limo plus tip	$400.00		$500.00	$400.00	$100.00	
22	Veil/Headpiece	$100.00		$150.00	$150.00	$0.00	
23	Shoes	$100.00		$150.00	$150.00	$0.00	
24	Escort Cards, Table Numbers, Food Labels	$100.00		$75.00	$75.00	$0.00	
25	Alterations	$250.00		$300.00	$0.00	$300.00	
26	Jewelry	$150.00		$200.00	$200.00	$0.00	
27	Marriage License(s)	$100.00		$100.00	$0.00	$100.00	
28	Card Box	$50.00		$50.00	$50.00	$0.00	
29	Bridal Party Gifts	$1,000.00		$750.00	$750.00	$0.00	
30	Parent Gifts	$500.00		$400.00	$400.00	$0.00	
31	Delivery Tips Day Of	$75.00		$50.00	$0.00	$50.00	
32	Slip/Petticoat	$100.00		$100.00	$100.00	$0.00	
33	Hotel Room	$200.00		$200.00	$200.00	$0.00	
34	Lingerie	$100.00		$125.00	$125.00	$0.00	
35	Totals:	$25,000.00		$28,430.00	$16,735.00	$11,695.00	
36							
37					Grand Total:	$28,430.00	

You can download a sample budget spreadsheet to edit, print and save at TheRealistBride.com/budget.

Obviously some of these items may not pertain to you, so you can eliminate the column or replace it with another miscellaneous item that's not listed.

Other things to consider in your wedding budget: additional stationery items, such as programs or menus; a guest book; gifts for you and your fiancé to give to each other; the rehearsal dinner, if parents aren't paying for it; beauty treatments, such as facials, massages, and mani/pedis; and prenuptial agreement lawyer fees. Honeymoon expenses, such as plane tickets, hotel rooms, tours, passport fees and spending money should have its own budget separate from your wedding.

4:

WEDDING COUNTDOWN TASK CHECKLIST

Here's a complete breakdown of what you have to do and how far in advance you need to do it.

12+ months

- Insure your engagement ring
- Choose a couple of wedding date options
- Create a budget
- Start putting together the guest list with your fiancé and your parents
- Visit potential venues and book your favorite
- Decide on who will be in your wedding party
- Choose your wedding colors
- Start your workout regimen and healthy eating
- Start researching vendors

9-11 months

- Book Your Photographer
- Order your wedding dress
- Finalize the guest list
- Book a caterer if food is not provided by your reception venue
- Hire a florist
- Hire a DJ or reception musicians
- Hire a videographer
- Register for gifts
- Book rental companies for chairs, linens, tableware, etc.
- Arrange hotel room blocks and book your room
- Book an officiant
- Order Save-the-Dates

6-9 months

- Mail Save-the-Dates (if you're having a destination wedding, mail these 9-12 months before your wedding)
- Book wedding day transportation
- Book ceremony musicians if you're having them
- Order bridesmaid and flower girl dresses
- Start planning your honeymoon
- Have your food tasting and select your reception menu
- Order wedding invitations

4-6 months

- Attend couples counseling if required by your ceremony site
- Shop for tuxes for groom, groomsmen and ring bearer
- Apply for or renew passports
- Order your wedding cake
- Hire your wedding day transportation
- Hire a calligrapher if you plan to use one
- Send your Maid of Honor your bridal shower guest list
- Purchase your wedding shoes
- Book appointments for hair and makeup trial and start saving inspiration pictures

2-3 months

- Attend your bridal shower
- Shop for wedding rings and get sized (If you want to get custom rings, you'll need to do this at least 6 months in advance)

- Mail your invitations
- Start a spreadsheet for RSVPs
- Finalize arrangement looks with your florist
- Choose ceremony readings
- Finalize honeymoon plans and book hotel and plane tickets
- Have your trial run for hair and makeup
- Book your wedding day for hair stylist and makeup artist
- Start taking notes and drawing inspiration for your vows
- Purchase gifts for parents, wedding party, and groom
- Have your first gown fitting 6-8 weeks before your wedding and purchase dress undergarments
- Purchase your wedding jewelry
- Order wedding favors, ring bearer box/pillow, and flower girl basket

3-6 weeks

- Mail bridal shower thank you notes
- Purchase your unity candle, aisle runner, guest book, card box, cake serving set, cake stand, cake topper and toasting flutes (some of these may not apply to you!)
- Purchase wedding lingerie
- Apply for a marriage license. Check with your local clerk's office for requirements and how long it's good for
- Go over itemized list with your vendors and get a final quote on how much you owe
- Send your DJ/band your final song list
- Give your coordinator your complete vendor list with contact information

- Create a wedding program if you're having one
- Send photographer the timeline and shot list
- Make a reservation for your rehearsal dinner
- Put together or purchase a Bridal Emergency Kit
- Contact guests who haven't RSVPed
- Send invitations for your rehearsal dinner

2 weeks

- Have your final gown fitting. Bring your Maid of Honor to learn how to bustle your dress after the ceremony. Bring your dress home and put it in a safe place
- Discuss with your mom and MOH whether or not you'll have something old, new, borrowed and blue
- Confirm your hotel room reservation
- Pick up your wedding rings
- Plan your seating chart and fill out/print escort/place cards
- Give your final head count to your venue and caterer
- Make final payments to all vendors

1 week

- Call all wedding vendors and confirm times they'll be at the venue the day of the wedding. Give them your venue coordinator's contact information
- Get your hair cut & colored
- Have your fiancé get a haircut
- Finish your vows
- Attend bachelor/bachelorette parties
- Get a facial

- Confirm your rehearsal dinner reservation
- Prepare your rehearsal dinner toast
- Make a list of who in the wedding party is walking with whom and in which order they'll walk

2-3 days

- Groom and groomsmen pick up their wedding wear
- Drop off escort cards, card box, menus, disposable cameras, favors, unity candle, aisle runner, cake topper, cake stand, toasting flutes, and any signs or photos for the day of the wedding to your venue coordinator
- Make a plan of who will drive you to the ceremony if the transportation isn't coming until later
- Email the wedding day itinerary to your wedding party and immediate family

The Day before

- Get your final manicure and pedicure
- Meet with wedding party, ushers, ceremony readers, immediate family, your officiant and/or your site coordinator at the ceremony site to do your dress rehearsal
- Give your marriage license to your officiant (If for some reason they can't come to the rehearsal, you can give it to them the day of the wedding)
- Attend rehearsal dinner
- Give wedding party and parents gifts at the rehearsal dinner
- Try your best to relax and get some sleep

The Day of

- Exchange gifts with your soon-to-be husband
- Get your hair and makeup done
- Refer to your day of checklist to make sure you have everything
- Check into your hotel
- Give wedding bands to the Best Man and Maid of Honor to hold during the ceremony
- Give someone you trust the tip envelopes to distribute

The Day After

- Return your fiancé's tux or have one of the groomsmen do it for him
- Open your gifts and take notes on who gave you what
- Pack for your honeymoon

After you return from the honeymoon

- Get your dress and bouquet preserved
- Change your name
- Send thank you cards
- Speak with your photographer to go over photos and albums
- Review your wedding vendors online
- Exchange/return unwanted or duplicate gifts

Don't let the checklist overwhelm you. Take it one task at a time. Go to TheRealistBride.com/checklist for a printable version of this list.

5:

CHOOSING YOUR WEDDING STYLE

Choosing the type of wedding that you want to have is one of the first decisions you should make after getting engaged. Think about what you want your wedding to feel like. Are you interested in a casual gathering or an elegant affair? What do you envision when you think of the 'perfect wedding'?

Deciding what type of vibe you want your wedding to have will help you decide which themes to choose from. The type of wedding you're having should dictate your entire planning process, from the date to the venue to the dress, so that everything is cohesive and looks tailored just for you. While some brides have had every detail planned out since they were little, most of us need a little assistance in coming up with ideas. Here's a starting point for different types of weddings:

Rustic Chic

Country girls, rejoice: rustic weddings are all the rage right now, and it's easy to see why. They're charming without being over the top, they're simple without being dull, and they have tons of affordable options for decor.

Venue types: A barn, a garden, a park, or a backyard.

Wedding dress: Lace gowns are made for romantic rustic weddings. Choose a fit and flare or A-line with medium to no train as trains do not fare well in outdoor settings.

Bridesmaid Dresses: Short and flirty in light fabrics. Rustic wedding themes are not usually formal and they also get pretty hot, so a short bridesmaid dress is the most appropriate for an outdoor wedding.

Wedding Color Ideas: Peach and grey, blush and white, and pink and grey are all romantic without being too formal.

Décor Inspiration: Peonies in mason jars, a chalkboard listing your signature drink, and sparklers for your guests to hold as you exit the ceremony.

Food Style: Upscale barbeque or comfort food in a buffet. One of the best things about a rustic wedding theme is that your guests will love the down-home feel of their favorite foods.

Beach or Destination Wedding

Some people were born to be beach bums. If I could, I'd spend every day seaside with a cocktail in hand, and I know I'm not alone in this! Beach weddings range from ultra casual to semi-formal and have a very peaceful feel. (Not to mention, your photos will be gorgeous.)

Venue: Your ceremony will obviously be at the beach, but try a reception space at a restaurant overlooking the water where you were just married. Some hotels have restaurants that are completely open and on the water, and others will set up your reception space right on the beach with tables under drapery.

Dress: Choose an ethereal dress with lightweight fabric. No ball gowns or trains...it will all get caught in the sand.

Bridesmaids: Short dresses in light fabrics, and nothing poofy. Depending how casual you want your wedding to be, a sundress could work.

Wedding Color Ideas: Tropical or ocean themed colors work best for beach weddings. Bright orange and purple, fuchsia and tangerine, turquoise and purple, aqua and white or an all white wedding all work.

Décor Inspiration: An altar draped in fabric, floating candles in water filled hurricane glasses, and authentic seashell favors from the beach or island where your ceremony is located.

Food Style: Because beach and destination weddings often have a much smaller guest list, dependent on your venue, you may be able to use a prix fixe menu (full course meal at a fixed price with options) that the guests can order from. Keep the menu light and fresh..it'll be too hot to eat heavy!

Modern Wedding

Young couples with a refined sense of style tend to lean toward having modern wedding themes. It's cool, it's fresh and it's yet to be overdone.

Venue: A bar or hotel rooftop in a major city or an industrial warehouse are great options.

The Dress: A short or long dress can work. If you go for a traditional length dress, choose something with tons of structure and clean lines. No matter the style, choose a luxe fabric such as silk or charmeuse.

Bridesmaids: Short cocktail dresses, but nothing poofy as that can be seen as a little too cutesy. Don't be afraid of shine.

Wedding Color Ideas: White and grey, black with hints of light yellow and light green, grey and orange, and slate and wine all complement each other nicely. Stay away from two bright colors together as it doesn't fit the modern theme.

Décor Inspiration: String lights, tons of high top tables, and paper lanterns. Keep everything simple and uncluttered.

Food Style: Tapas (tons of small plate options) is all the rage right now. Finish the evening with a late night pizza snack.

Vintage Hollywood Glam

If you're thinking of having a vintage wedding theme, you are probably the type of person who loves a dramatic event...one with style, and a sparkle of old Hollywood glamour. If you're into the type of parties that Gatsby would throw, this could be the perfect wedding theme for you.

Venue Types: The venue should be fit for Hollywood royalty circa 1920. An historic theatre or library or an art gallery have culture and class and fit perfectly with a vintage wedding.

Wedding Dress: Depending what type of vintage you're going for, you can go ball gown or A-line (for Hollywood glam) or column Art Deco style full of beadwork (for a 20s feel.) Look for a gown with medium to no train as a long train doesn't go well with these types of venues.

Bridesmaid Dresses: Long & shimmery in black or metallics. Nothing beats a show-stopping art deco bridesmaid dress.

Wedding Colors: Rose gold and blush, gold and white, black and gold. Are you sensing a pattern? Gold is the way to go.

Décor Inspiration: Candelabra centerpieces, sparkling tablecloths and a vintage head piece. Special events used to be quite glamorous in old Hollywood, so yours should be too.

Food Style: Passed hors d'oeuvres and a plated meal since this is a formal wedding theme.

Travel Themed Wedding

Travel themed weddings are for the ones with wanderlust…the couples who can never visit enough countries and can never gain enough experiences. From the ancient history of Rome to the iconic romance of Paris to the spirituality of Bali, a travel themed wedding has endless possibilities.

Venue: You can travel to your destination or you can bring it to you. Find a place in your state that has a ton of history or culture. A large city's cultural center or an art gallery featuring works from around the world could work.

Dress: Any dress will work for this theme. If you're doing a vintage travel theme, try an authentic vintage dress. If you're going more modern, choose a sleek design with a rich fabric.

Bridesmaids: For a more upscale venue, choose a long dress, and for a more casual venue, go short. If you're sticking to one particular country for your theme, choose outfits that reflect the local culture.

Décor Inspiration: Vintage globes as centerpieces, a large map as a guest book that you can later have framed, and a sign that says "Our Love Knows No Bounds."

Food Style: Tapas is a great way to have tons of small options so you can have many courses as they do in many cultures, and it also gives the opportunity to sample from around the world (just make sure they complement each other). Spanish, Indian, Italian, French… there is no limit to your options, so be creative!

Elegant Wedding

When you think of your wedding and you envision a chic and classic affair with tons of little details that put it a step up from the average wedding, then you're probably going to want an elegant wedding.

Venue types: A ballroom or Country Club sets the right tone.

Wedding Dress: Elegant wedding dresses can be anywhere from chic with a touch of drama to an avant garde statement dress. A ball gown, A-line, or Fit & Flare will work, and a long train is appropriate.

Bridesmaids: Long dresses are more appropriate unless you choose a very fancy cocktail dress.

Wedding Color Ideas: Classic colors work best. Use black as one of your colors as it exudes elegance and will never go out of style. Red and black, black and white, and black and gold are all great options.

Décor Inspiration: Chiavari chairs, tall floral centerpieces and draping or a rented chandelier. The more avant garde, the better.

Food Style: Plated options with multiple courses. Place menus explaining each dish in detail at each person's seat.

Romantic

If you're interested in a romantic wedding, you're probably a dreamer, and perhaps your biggest dream is about your wedding day. The whole event should have an delicate feel, from the floral arrangements to the wedding gown.

Venue Types: A hotel ballroom, a vineyard, a castle or estate are all great choices. Somewhere enchanting and alluring will fit best.

Dress: You have lots of dress options that correspond with a romantic wedding theme, including a ball gown with tulle, a lace A-line, or a fit and flare. Any size train is appropriate, but if the venue is outside, you'll probably want to skip the train.

Bridesmaid Dresses: Long and flowy in organza and chiffon fabrics are dreamy and romantic.

Wedding Colors: Blush and ivory, light pink and gold, lilac and ivory, and tiffany blue and light gold. Keeping wedding colors light exudes romance.

Décor Inspiration: Tons of candles in alternating short and tall jars lining the aisle, a directional sign to guide your wedding guests, and your favorite quotes about love as part of the centerpiece at each table.

Food Style: The venues for romantic wedding themes tend to be upscale, so you should have a plated meal with passed hors d'oeuvres.

Fall Wedding

There's something about fall that's very romantic...the leaves are changing colors into beautiful reds and yellows, and the weather is just right for cozying up in a sweatshirt. Fall wedding themes are great because you (and your wedding party) don't have to deal with extreme heat or extreme cold.

Venue: If your wedding is in early fall or you live in a state with a mild autumn, consider having it at an outdoor setting to capture the colors, such as at a park or a cider mill. Country clubs or a rented restaurant overlooking tons of trees are great options for receptions in colder autumn months.

Wedding Colors: Go for rich colors that complement each other. Tangerine and chocolate brown, eggplant and pumpkin, and cranberry and bronze all work.

The Dress: If your wedding is outdoors, a lace fit and flare or A-line is a great option. If the wedding is indoors, lucky you! Pretty much any style of wedding gown works from ball gowns to mermaids.

Bridesmaids: Long dresses are the best option for bridesmaids for a fall wedding theme. Fabrics like chiffon, satin, and charmeuse are great for the weather.

Décor Inspiration: Tree branches sticking out of floral centerpieces, lanterns holding candles, and personalized mason jars full of pumpkin butter as a wedding favor.

Food Style: This will depend on your setting. For an outdoor/less formal event, buffet style (hot) comfort foods are a great option with caramel apples for dessert. For a more upscale event, plated meals are appropriate. Consider serving hot cider with cinnamon sticks during cocktail hour.

Nautical

Do you and your fiancé love spending every free moment on a boat? Do the waves crashing and the big open water speak to your soul? A nautical wedding theme could be the perfect way to combine your love for your future spouse and your love for the water.

Venues: A yacht club, sailing club, or on a boat.

The Dress: If you're having your wedding on a boat, a column dress or fit and flare are best; a large ball gown will be hard to maneuver in.

Bridesmaids: The bridesmaid dresses will depend on how formal your event is. For an event on the water, short bridal gowns are the best choice. If you're having a formal event in a yacht club, you can go for short or long dresses.

Wedding Colors: Navy and ivory, red and navy, and navy and gold all have a nautical feel.

Décor Inspiration: Mini lighthouse centerpieces, rope knot place card holders, and message in a bottle favors thanking your guests for attending.

Food Style: Given the venue options, you will most likely have a buffet. Don't serve anything with a strong smell as it may make your guests nauseated if they're on a boat.

Whimsical

Whimsical wedding themes are perfect for couples who don't take themselves too seriously. These weddings tend to be more casual and are more about having a blast and celebrating your love than they are about being fancy. Whimsical weddings are probably the most fun to plan because of just that...they're fun and playful.

Venue Types: A public park, an English style garden, a bed & breakfast, or a backyard wedding can all accommodate this theme. Quirky locations work best.

Wedding Colors: Bright colors work great for whimsical wedding themes. Orange and aqua; aqua and coral; and yellow and light blue all work. If they complement each other, try mixing your favorite color and his favorite color.

Wedding Dress: Short, tea-length or long, in any fit from a bridal salon or department store all work! Wear what makes you feel beautiful.

Bridesmaid Dresses: Short dresses are appropriate in light fabrics such as cotton or jersey.

Décor Inspiration: A chalkboard sign for seating, an arch altar made of tree branches and flowers, and paper lanterns to let go of at the end of the night.

Food Style: Buffet style. If your venue allows it, try a DIY bar where you supply the liquor and mixers and everyone can make their own cocktails. (Never have a BYOB event!)

Winter Wonderland

Part of what makes a winter wedding so romantic is that it has that 'magic' feel, especially in the snow. Getting married in the wintertime has its advantages; sometimes the venue is less expensive because you're not in the typical "wedding season", which also means you won't be overlapping with your friends' weddings!

Venue: A formal ballroom or a ski lodge are great options for winter weddings. For a more intimate feel, rent out a property with a lodge and multiple cabins. That way you can have the wedding, reception and sleeping quarters all in one place!

Dress: Go for a ball gown and a faux fur bolero and muff to keep warm without compromising style.

Bridesmaid Dresses: Long dresses in heavy fabrics such as silk, satin or even lace with any sleeve length.

Wedding Color Ideas: Any shade of blue and silver, dark purple or lilac and silver, deep red and gold, maroon and dark blue, or all ivory.

Décor Inspiration: Faux tree branches spray painted frosty white, tall glass floral centerpieces with crystals hanging like chandeliers, and sheer white drapery hanging from the ceiling.

Food Style: Dependent on your venue you may have it catered or your venue may supply the food. Try to do a plated meal as winter weddings are typically formal.

Fairytale

This theme is for ladies who envision being seen as royalty for the day. A fairytale wedding theme brings together the opulence of medieval times with the romance of A Midsummer Night's Dream.

Venue: Your venue should be large and grand. If you can swing a castle, that's your best option. (There are some castles in the US!) If not, a sprawling, old estate with indoor and outdoor space is also a great choice.

The Dress: This is your moment, and your dress should be fit for a queen. Ball gowns in luxe fabrics like silk or satin work best for fairytale wedding themes. Use a large petticoat to make it even more dramatic.

Bridesmaids: Long dresses are the only regal choice. Consider ethereal fabrics such as chiffon or organza.

Wedding Color Ideas: Royal blue and gold, deep plum and gold, red and black, and purple and silver are all great options.

Décor Inspiration: A sign that says Happily Ever After Starts Here and a storybook beginning with Once Upon a Time featuring your photos as a couple used as a guestbook. Consider long banquet tables with tall candelabras instead of traditional round tables.

Food Style: Try a renaissance approach with family style meals with tons of options, including bread, fruit, a main course, a dessert, and wine to go with the meal.

Whichever type of wedding you choose to have, just make sure it reflects you and your fiancé's tastes and what you love. If you need help looking for decor and favors that follow your wedding theme, visit TheRealistBride.com for assistance and more inspiration.

Don't worry about what your parents and your guests think you should do. It's your day; have the kind of wedding that speaks to you.

6:

THE GUEST LIST

The guest list was probably the most agonizing part of planning our wedding. Between cutting people we wanted to invite and pissing off our parents by not inviting people we didn't care about that they somehow deemed essential, it's a lot to take in. And that's not even considering the guests themselves.

First there was someone whom we weren't sure if were inviting who said "I will definitely be there." Then there was "when can we book our room?" from a couple on our "maybe" list. Lastly, there was a couple, whom I had never met, who straight up asked Joey if they could come. I'm not sure what gives people this sense of entitlement, but it happens.

People will tell you "It's your wedding. Do what makes you happy." The people who say this are very sweet and they are not immediate family. Parents do not ASK about people they want invited (though they should)...they EXPECT people to be invited.

Creating Your Wedding Guest List

The easiest way to cut down on budget is to cut the guest list. You'll save on food and beverage, invitations, centerpieces and favors, so it's a pretty huge savings. (Just don't get so carried away trying to save money that you exclude people who really should be there.)

The first thing you and your fiancé should do is set a maximum number of total guests you'd like to invite.

Don't just pick a number out of the air; consider how much each guest is going to cost you, how many people the kind of venue you want holds, and if you want to have a huge or an intimate wedding. Count on between 10-20% of invited guests to decline, so if you invite 100 total guests, expect 80 - 90 of them to accept.

Next, make an all inclusive list with your fiancé of everyone you think might be a possibility: friends, relatives, co-workers, and parents' friends. Divide your list into three categories: Must Invite, Maybe, and Okay Not to Invite.

Then, ask for a list from each of your parents of who they'd like invited. Be sure to let them know that this is a "wish list" and does not guarantee an invitation. Compare with your list and decide who from their list should be added and who shouldn't.

The guest list is something that you'll go over together as a couple, then go over with your parents, then revise, and revise, and revise until it's time to send Save-the-Dates. Start with everyone and whittle it down from there.

The rules are daunting as to who you have to invite, but contrary to what some people believe, you do NOT have to give everyone a plus one (and you shouldn't...it's way too expensive!) Some basic rules and etiquette for creating your guest list:

- If someone is married or engaged, you must invite their spouse/future spouse. It doesn't matter if you've never met their significant other. They're a team now, and where one

41

goes, the other must also be allowed to go. You might get lucky and the person you want to invite will come alone, but you have to give them the option.

- The same rule goes for people living together. Couples who cohabitate should be treated as a team as well, for they are in a very serious relationship.

- You don't have to invite everyone's significant other. Judge it on a case by case basis. If they just started dating, you don't have to invite the guest's SO, especially if you haven't met them. If they've been together for at least a year, or if you've met their SO more than a few times, you should invite them as a couple.

- Try to give guests who won't know anyone at your reception a plus one. You don't want them sitting by themselves with no one to talk to; you want everyone having fun! If there's a one-off person who truly doesn't know anyone else, it's a nice gesture to give them a plus one, even if they're single.

- As a general rule of thumb, you should try to give the people in your wedding party a plus one. Sometimes this isn't feasible within your budget, so don't feel bad about it; they're going to be sitting away from their date at the head table anyway. Just make sure you give every person in your party a plus one or none of them at all (besides the serious relationship/married people.)

- Don't feel obligated to invite people just because you were invited to their wedding. If you aren't especially close with the couple anymore and don't see them often, it's okay not to invite them. It's totally your call.

- Think about each couple and how often you currently interact. Would you call them up, today, and ask them to hang out? People drift apart. If you haven't spoken to them in over a year and you aren't related to them, it's perfectly acceptable not to invite them.

- It's okay not to invite kids to your wedding, but be prepared for family to get miffed about it. If you don't want children to come, only address invitations to people over age 18, and ask your parents to spread the word that it's an 'adults only' wedding. Don't write "no kids" on the invitation- that's seen as bad taste. If someone RSVPs their child, pick up the phone and politely explain to the parents that due to budget, you've decided to only invite adults to your wedding, and that you'd love it if they could still make it.

- As soon as regrets start to come in, mail your 'maybe' invitations out. (Just don't wait too long; you don't want them to know they were on the B list.)

- If the wedding and reception are the same day, then anyone who is invited to the wedding should be invited to the reception, and vice versa.

- If you invite a first relative, you must invite their siblings. If you invite some first cousins, then you're going to have to invite all first cousins. If you're not close with any of your cousins and you're trying to majorly cut down your list, consider not inviting any cousins.

If you and your fiancé are paying for the wedding, you technically do not have to invite anyone you don't want to invite. Sometimes it is better, though, to make small concessions (if you can afford it) to avoid family dramas.

If your parents are paying for or contributing a large portion to the wedding, you will probably have to make more concessions for guests than you want to. This does not, however, give your parents carte blanche with the guest list. It's still YOUR wedding. Use guest number limitations as an out. If the venue only allows 150 and your list is at 175, it's time to make some cuts. (They don't need to know that your venue actually holds 200.)

I tried to make everyone as happy as possible. We didn't invite 100% of the people that our parents wanted invited but we did invite most of them. You're never going to make every person happy unless you invite every person on their list...and maybe not even then, so just do what you and your fiancé think is right.

7:

BOOKING A VENUE

Nothing sets the stage for what type of wedding you're having more than the wedding and reception venue. Try to meet with the site coordinator on a day that a wedding will be taking place so you can get an idea of what the set up might look like. If possible, I highly recommend having your ceremony and reception at the same venue because it is extremely convenient.

What to ask:

Is your venue available on these dates? Go in with a few dates and times in mind and see what they have available.

Does the space offer food? If so, what is the price per plate, and what are the options? Is there a food tasting? Do they have buffet or plated options? Is there a wide variety of food that sounds good to you? Is the price within your budget? I recommend only choosing a venue (or caterer) that allows you to taste the food before deciding on a final menu.

If you offer food, will you allow outside catering, and will they have access to the kitchen? Most places that offer food won't allow outside catering, so if you have your heart set on a certain caterer, check with the venue before booking anything.

Do you have options for guests with dietary restrictions? You should be asking this of whomever is providing the food. If you have guests with dietary restrictions, such as gluten intolerant or vegan, you **have** to feed them something they can eat. You don't have to serve that as one of your food options as long as you make certain you can have an accommodation made for them the day of the reception.

If you don't offer food, do you have a list of preferred caterers? This is a great way to start your list of caterers to check out, and if it's on their preferred list, that means they've worked with them before.

Do I *have* to choose vendors off of your preferred list? Try to steer clear of this; you're paying for it, so you should be allowed to choose your own vendors.

Are tables, linens, chairs, chair covers, and tableware provided, or do I have to rent them? If they are provided, what do they look like? Though most of these may be included, they could be super ugly or dated. Always ask to see what everything looks like so you can get an idea of if you'd have to rent any items.

Do you charge a cake cutting fee? Most venues charge a cake cutting fee of $1-$2 per guest if the cake is made by a baker offsite. If the venue is making the cake, they should be able to waive this fee, especially because the top tier of the cake is usually the only part that's real! (It all looks real, but it's often Styrofoam so that the real cake can be cut easily in the back.)

Is there a room rental fee? Some venues don't just charge for food; they put a price on renting the room itself out.

What other fees are there? There may be cleaning fees, set up/tear down fees, and/or service charges. Get a complete list and what each fee covers.

For outdoor spaces: What's the plan if it rains? No one can predict the weather. You should always have a backup plan in place.

For fall/winter weddings: Is there a coat check service? It's necessary for guests to have somewhere to put their coats. This may add an additional service charge.

How many people can the space accommodate? Many venues have a strict guest limit, so be sure it's in line with your guest list count.

Do you have a minimum spend requirement? Some venues have a food and/or drink minimum, so make sure your number of guests will be able to meet it so you don't end up paying extra for nothing.

Is there a coordinator available to be my contact, and if so, is there an additional cost for that? You're going to want to have one main point of contact to ask questions as they arise, to be there the day of the wedding, and to coordinate with your vendors.

How many events are taking place the day I want to have my wedding? If there's more than one event going on, you'll need to put up signs to direct your guests to the proper room.

Do you have ceremony as well as reception space? If so, is there a bride's area to get ready? How much does each space cost?

How big is the dance floor? What if they have a beautiful space with a tiny dance floor? That's not conducive to people dancing!

What does the restroom look like? It may sound strange, but you don't want a dumpy (no pun intended) looking bathroom for a nice wedding. Make sure there's enough stalls to accommodate your guests.

What restrictions do you have? Most venues have some sort of restrictions; find out if real candles are allowed, and if you can hang anything off the walls or the ceiling, such as drapery or chandeliers.

Can we bring our own alcohol? The bar charge can be pretty steep for receptions, so you can try to cut costs by asking if you can supply your own beverages. Just remember that it's one more thing to add to your to-do list, and you might be faced with the problem of running out of drinks.

If drinks are included, how long do we have an open bar? Find out how many hours of open bar are included in your package. We saved ourselves from being charged an extra hour by closing the bar during dinner. You'll also want to see how late the venue is allowed to serve alcohol; some states require venues to stop serving alcohol for at least 30 minutes before the event concludes.

What time do people have to leave at the end of the night? If you're planning on raging until 1am, make sure you have the space that late.

Does the venue have liability insurance? Receptions can get pretty wild, and if someone gets injured on the dance floor, you don't want to be held responsible.

How much of a deposit do you require to book? What's the payment plan? Usually a large deposit is required to book the space. Find out how their payment structure works, and the date your final head count/payment is due.

What is your cancellation policy? Find out if any of your money is refundable, if there's a charge to change the date, and at what point you need to cancel in order to get your money back.

If you're working with a tight budget, ask what kind of discounts are offered for weddings on Fridays and Sundays (Saturdays are the most expensive day to host weddings.) You should also ask if they have cheaper rates for "off-season" weddings November through March.

Your final payment to your venue and/or caterer will likely be due two weeks before the wedding. When giving final numbers, don't forget to include you and your fiancé, as well as any vendors who require a meal.

8:

CHOOSING AND LOSING BRIDESMAIDS

Putting together your bridal party is tricky. You don't want to leave people out, and you also don't want to make people feel obligated. Guess what? You're entitled to ask whomever you want- no more, no less- to be a part of your wedding party. (If they don't want to do it, they can say no.) Keep in mind that the larger your bridal party gets, the more expensive it becomes for you, but a super small bridal party gives each bridesmaid more responsibility and more financial obligations. It's all about balance. For me, five was the perfect number.

When you think about your bridal party, think not just of who you hang out with the most, but who you can trust, who is responsible, and who is going to be so happy for you that they only want you to have the most special day. If you have a friend that you'd like to be a part of your day but aren't sure they're up to the task of being a bridesmaid, ask them to read something at the ceremony.

Here's a guideline of what your bridesmaids' duties should entail:

- Shopping for a bridesmaid dress (with a good attitude), purchasing it and accompanying shoes in a timely fashion.
- Planning, paying for, and attending your bridal shower. Planning includes finding and securing

a place, purchasing and/or creating centerpieces, coming up with fun games, and running the show the day of.

- Planning your bachelorette party and buying the favors. Be clear about what you want to do, if you want to do a joint party with your fiancé, and whether or not you're down with male strippers. (Spoiler Alert: they don't all look as good as the guys in *Magic Mike.*)
- Attending the dress rehearsal and dinner afterward.
- Paying for hair and makeup on the wedding day. (If for some reason you want to do a bridesmaid trial, that's something you're going to have to pay for.)
- Assisting you with Day Of Wedding duties- you can see a complete list of these on my blog, TheRealistBride.com.

Your Maid of Honor should be a person you're close to and trust the most to help you with a variety of tasks. Maid of Honor duties include all of the above, plus:

- Keeping a list of who gave you what gifts during your bridal shower.
- Attending bridal gown shopping and fittings with you.
- Being the leader of the bridesmaids: keeping everything organized for the bridal shower and bachelorette party, making sure the other bridesmaids have purchased their dresses and

shoes in a timely fashion, and putting a stop to any problems or dramas that may come up.

- Signing your marriage certificate as a witness.
- Assisting with bustling your dress after the ceremony. If your dress has a train, it needs to be bustled before the reception. At your last fitting, have the seamstress show her how to do it and let her practice a couple of times.
- Giving a toast at the reception.
- Being your biggest advocate. Maid of Honors become quasi therapists during your engagement period. You're going to have moments where you scream and/or cry, and not only should they allow you to vent, they should help you in any way that they possibly can.

What your bridesmaids are not: slaves. Bridesmaids need to be available to you, but that doesn't mean that their lives get put on hold just because you're getting married.

Do not:

- Assume they are available to you 24/7. Everyone has their own shit going on. Be reasonable about how much you're asking of their time.
- Ask them to greatly alter their appearance for your wedding. (If you want a friend to temporarily take out piercings or cover tattoos,

this is okay. I had a friend in a bridal party where the bride requested that all bridesmaids dye their hair blond- this is not okay.)

- Become a bridezilla. Your bridesmaids are your friends; treat them as such.

If you feel you've been asking for help within reason and you haven't been getting the help you need, you need to address it directly and in person. The entire reason bridesmaids exist is so that they can help you during this stressful time.

You Have a Problem Bridesmaid

If you've chosen your bridal party, then you already know what I'm talking about. You have a bridesmaid that is a problem child who just can't seem to grow up. It could be that they are starting drama with your other bridesmaids; it could be that they haven't been showing up on time (or at all) to important wedding related events; it could be that they started to become an absentee friend as soon as you gave them a job to do (being a bridesmaid is a job, not just a title.) This person might even be your Maid of Honor. Do yourself a favor and **get rid of them.** (Don't kill them, obviously. Just kick them out of your wedding party. And possibly out of your life.)

You have enough to worry about financially and emotionally; you don't need the added stress of someone acting like a dumb B. Ask yourself one question: am I asking too much of my bridesmaids? If the answer is no, it's time to make a change.

Weddings are not just about you and your fiancé. They're about all of the relationships in your life, including your relatives and your best friends, and you will never have a better grasp on where you stand with someone than you will after you get engaged.

So, how do I know you have a problem bridesmaid? Because **everyone** has one.

Let me tell you a story:

I had a bridesmaid that, before I even asked her to be in my wedding, I knew might drop out at some point. There's your first clue that I should have trusted my instincts and not asked her.

I asked her anyway because we had been friends for over 15 years and we had a lot of fun together. Unfortunately a long standing friendship doesn't necessarily make a good bridesmaid.

After complaining about her financial struggles several times to my other bridesmaids, I let her know that she didn't have to be in the wedding if it was too much for her, but she said she wanted to make it work. Then she no call, no showed for bridesmaid dress shopping, basically ruining my mood before we even started. The reason she gave ended up being legitimate, (though there was no reason she couldn't call) but because of the nature of the things that were happening in her life, I told her that it would probably be most mutually beneficial if she attended the wedding as a guest. I thought that she would take my SECOND offer to drop out of the wedding with no hard feelings attached on either side. Instead she explained that she was honored that I had asked her to be in the wedding and really wanted to be a part of it. Because this was not just affecting my own stress level and budget, but also affecting my bridesmaids deciding where I could have my bridal shower and when it could be booked, I asked for her to give me a final answer by the end of the week. So here I am, giving my time to this, stressing about the situation instead of receiving help from this person. People were telling me to not give her the option but I was trying to be fair. I gave her a deadline of that Friday because my MOH was trying to put a down payment on a shower location that Saturday.

Friday came and went. An entire **week** after she was supposed to get back to me, she sent me an email saying: "I tried emailing you but I guess it didn't go through, and I am assuming it is too late now to be in it." She didn't even have the decency to come up with a good lie.

No one can possibly know how tough it is to plan a wedding until they are in the position themselves. There are so many things to worry about and a bridesmaid should not be one of them. The moral of the story is if you have a selfish friend, don't ask them to be a bridesmaid, because expecting them to act differently just because you're getting married is setting yourself up for failure.

Bridesmaid Dress Shopping

You should start shopping for bridesmaid dresses at least six months before your wedding. It takes a few months for them to come in, and you'll need to allow time for alterations. I'll be honest; it's pretty fun ordering your friends to try on only dresses that you like. Make a day of the shopping and go out to eat afterward. It's a bonding experience and a great way for bridesmaids who don't know each other well to get acquainted.

Look for a salon with a good variety of dresses that your bridesmaids can afford. I have expensive taste, leaving me with an internal battle between what I wanted and what I thought everyone in the wedding party would be happy with. If money were not an issue, they would have all worn Monique Lhuillier gowns. But this is reality, and money IS an issue for most people, and you have to respect that not everyone wants to spend a million dollars on YOUR wedding. If money isn't an issue for you and you want your bridesmaids wearing top of the line designer gowns, you should pay for them. It's expensive enough as it is to be in a wedding, so try to be mindful of that.

The latest trend is to have bridesmaids wear all different dresses, and sometimes they even get to choose their own dress. I get the idea, but I personally think the wedding looks much more cohesive and elegant with the dresses being the same. It's also really fun looking at the dance floor and immediately being able to identify who was in the wedding party. You'll have to think about the kind of wedding you're having and decide for yourself if matching bridesmaid dresses are the right choice or not.

Remember to have ALL of your bridesmaids try on the dresses you are considering for them. Everyone's body type is unique and the dress can look completely different from one person to the next. I don't believe in making bridesmaids look bad so that the bride stands out. I think that whole philosophy is a little psychotic.

9:

CHOOSING YOUR VENDORS

The Photographer

Besides the venue, the most important selection you'll make about your wedding day is the photographer. This is not where you want to skimp on price! The photos will last a lifetime and be the best reminder of everything that happened on one of the biggest days of your life. If the photos are out of focus, unflattering, or have bad editing, that's all you're going to see when you look at them. You should book your photographer a minimum of nine months in advance, but a year in advance is ideal. High demand photographers should be booked as soon as possible. You don't want the leftover photographers. Deposits for booking photographers are usually 1/3 to 1/2 of the total price. Allot 10-15% of your budget for photography (or more, if this is the most important budget item to you.)

Photographers are artists, and each one has their own individual style, so you should spend some time taking a look at what they have available on their website to get a feel for their work. Once you've found some that you like and they've confirmed that they're available on your wedding date and within your budget, set up a meeting and go over these questions.

Do you have a portfolio I can look at? If they don't, run for the hills. When they present you with their portfolio, it should be clean and professional and showcase their work, and they should be showing you photos from a variety of weddings. Remember that they are probably showing you some of their best stuff, so if you aren't impressed, this isn't the photographer for you.

How long will you be there the day of the wedding? Their contract should outline exactly how many hours they are made available to you. Be sure there's enough time for photos before the wedding, during dancing at the reception, and all the way until you cut the cake and toss the bouquet. Eight hours is standard.

If I want you to stay longer, how much do you charge? Sometimes the party is hopping, and sometimes things just take longer than you expected, so get an idea of how much the overage charge is if you want them to stay longer than the contract allows.

Are you the photographer who will shoot us? If you're meeting with a large company, they designate photographers to each event, so you'll want to make sure the person you're meeting is actually the person who will be taking your photos. I recommend going with a photographer who owns their company; they have the most invested financially and emotionally and I think they do a better job.

Can I give you a list of shots that I want? Part of your photographer's job is to capture candid moments and put together creative shots of you, your family and your bridal party. However, if there's a couple of specific photo setups that you have in mind, ask if they're cool with that.

How many weddings do you do in a day? Their answer should be one. It's a full day of work. If they're squeezing in two, that's how things are forgotten and work is rushed.

What's the backup plan if you're sick? They should have a go-to photographer on standby in case of an emergency. Get the name so you can check their stuff out as well.

What packages do you offer? Some photographers don't include printed images at all and you have to buy everything ala carte; some provide just a few prints; some will either give you an album of your photos or charge a fee for it. Be sure to consider all of this in your photography budget, and if they do put together an album, ask if you or they select the photos that are used for it.

Do you edit/retouch/color correct? A professional won't just take photos, but will edit them as well. If you want something specific done, they'll likely charge extra for it (like photoshopping someone completely out of a photo, which our photographer told us he had been asked to do).

What types of paper do you use for prints and albums, and is there an upcharge for certain kinds? They may be showing you albums that have the highest quality paper, which will cost extra. Make sure that all of your photos will be on acid free paper so that they'll last without degrading over time.

What's the payment schedule? This should be laid out in your contract. Some photographers do payments in thirds, and some do them in halves. Check to see when each payment is due.

What is your cancellation policy? Check if any deposits are refundable in case you have to change your wedding date and they aren't available or something happens and you have to cancel.

Do we get a copy of the negatives and/or digital images? Make sure you're able to get a copy of these so you can have the images stored for any later use, including getting copies printed, and ask if they charge extra for this.

Do you do engagement photos? The best practice for wedding photos and getting to know your photographer is to book them for engagement photos. Ask if the price is included, and if not, how much they charge. (It should be significantly less than wedding photos.)

Who gets the rights to the images? Some photographers (including mine) own the rights to your images and are able to use and distribute them as they wish. This also means that you cannot distribute to magazines or blogs/profit from them without permission. If you plan on sharing the images on social media, you may also need their permission for that. Ours just asked us to credit him each time we posted one.

Photography Timeline

Once it gets close to your wedding day, your photographer will most likely ask you to fill in a timeline so that they know what's happening where and when. Here's a sample photography timeline:

8 Hours Photography Coverage

Sample Timeline for Wedding at 5pm

Ceremony location:

ABC Church

123 Main St.

Detroit, MI 48224

Reception location:

XYZ Ballroom

555 Main St.

Detroit, MI 48226

3:00pm: Photographer arrives. Allow at least two hours before the ceremony so you can get photos with bridesmaids, groomsmen, and parents. Specify if you'll be doing "first look" shots with your fiancé (photos of them seeing you in your dress for the first time prior to the ceremony).

5:00pm: Ceremony begins. List any specific shots you want of your ceremony space. You don't have to specify getting shots with your fiancé or the person walking you down the aisle unless you have something specific in mind.

5:30-7:00pm: Cocktail hour. Leave 1.5 hours minimum between your ceremony and reception so you have enough time for formal shots and any offsite photos, and remember to allow for drive time. Arrange for the photographer to join you in your transportation to offsite locations.

- **Formal portraits**

-Bride & groom
-Group shots of families with bride & groom
-Wedding party
List any specific shots you want

- **Offsite locations**
List address and any specific shots you want

7:00 pm: Reception begins

Grand entrance: 7:05pm
Cake Cutting: 7:15pm
First dance: 8:30pm
Father/daughter dance: 8:35pm
Mother/son dance: 8:40pm
Bouquet toss: 10pm
List any specific shots you want of certain people and/or decor

11:00pm: Photographer departs

Just as important as a photographer's work is their personality. This is someone you'll be spending all day with and be taking direction from, so make sure you and your fiancé are comfortable with them and that they listen to your needs.

The Florist

A wedding florist is a little more than somewhere to get your flowers. They completely transform the space, creating the look of your entire event. With this responsibility comes a high price tag. It's warranted, though, because they have to order flowers, take the time with you to design your wedding and reception look, coordinate with your planner and/or the venue, and set up/take down the day of the event. It usually takes a few people to make this happen, and they have to pay their employees. Truth be told, I didn't realize how much goes into a centerpiece; it's a lot more than just putting flowers in a vase.

That said, there are a few ways to cut down on your floral expenses.

Choose flowers in season. If you choose a flower that's harder for the florist to get, you're going to have to pay extra. Visit my blog at TheRealistBride.com for a chart of which flowers are in season during your wedding.

Use short centerpieces or alternate between tall and short. I wanted a dramatic look at my wedding, and nothing says drama like a tall centerpiece. I couldn't afford it for every table, so I ended up alternating between short and tall and it looked great.

Use greenery. Greens are much less expensive than flowers and they take up a lot of space in an arrangement.

Skip groomsmen boutonnières. Try a nice pocket square instead and reserve boutonnières for parents and grandparents only.

Only use flowers at the ceremony. There's no rule that says you have to have floral centerpieces at your reception. Most floral designers have other centerpieces, such as candelabras, that you can rent that are a cheaper alternative.

Use your bouquets at the head table. Talk to your florist about this...they do it all the time. They'll put out vases with water where you and your bridesmaids can stick your bouquets, and voila! No extra centerpieces needed at the head table unless you want them.

Use fake petals for the flower girl. No one can tell the difference, and bonus, they won't stain the bottom of your dress when you're walking down the aisle.

Don't go H.A.M. on your bouquet. Your bouquet should be larger and slightly different than your bridesmaids' bouquets, but that doesn't mean you need cascading flowers or one so large it blocks your entire dress. The smaller and simpler the bouquet, the less expensive it will be.

As always, do your research before selecting a vendor. Choose someone you like, too, because you're going to be spending a lot of time with them, and you want someone who is going to listen to what your vision is and execute it to perfection. Meet with at least three floral vendors before putting down a deposit. Deposits to hold the date range from $100 to 50% of the total floral budget; it completely depends on the vendor.

As far as budget goes, the florist will ask you how much you are planning on spending on flowers before they put together an itemized list and give you a quote. You should allot 10% of your total wedding budget to flowers/décor for the ceremony and reception.

If you're thinking to yourself, "I'm going to save money by doing the flowers myself!" Let me stop you right there. Do you really want to be worrying about picking up flowers and setting up centerpieces while you're supposed to be getting ready? Or taking everything down at the end of the night when you're dog tired? What if there's a problem and you can't get the flowers you want? What if the flowers are in bad shape and start to wilt?

Your time has value. I tell this to people in my life all the time. The cheapest way is never the simplest way, and you need to consider the time you give as an investment. If it's not worth the time investment, it's not worth it, period.

Questions You Should Ask Floral Designers

- **Do you have my date open?** Most florists do more than one wedding per day, so they should be able to make it work. Just make sure they aren't vacationing that day or something.
- **Is my budget going to work?** Some florists have minimum budgets, so you'll want to make sure that it's in line with what you're willing to spend. You also want to make sure they can do what you're asking for within your budget. If your taste isn't in line with your wallet, they should be able to make recommendations on how to keep certain elements the way you want while changing others to bring the cost down.
- **What's your style?** If your style is modern and their style is traditional, your arrangements probably aren't going to look the way you envision them looking, so choose a designer with similar taste to yours.
- **Do you have a portfolio I can look at?** Pictures speak the loudest when it comes to floral designers. If the centerpieces look cheap, mismatched, or the flowers don't look healthy, move on.
- **Do you do custom packages or do I have to choose from a certain package?** Custom is the way to go so you get exactly what you want.
- **Will you work with my cake designer if I decide to add flowers to my wedding cake?**

You'll want to know if they accommodate this, and how much they charge to do it.

- **How many events do you do per day? Are you personally going to be there to set up my wedding?** You want to be sure you're getting attention from your actual designer and not just a team that they assign to your wedding. Don't hire a designer who does more than a few weddings per day, as they will not have time to make sure everything is as it should be before moving on to the next event.
- **Are you available to do a walk-through of my event space prior to the wedding?** Hint: the answer should be yes. A real designer will want to look at the space to gain inspiration and get a better vision of how you want the space to look.
- **Can you move the flowers from the ceremony to the reception?** People don't realize this, but if you use floral altar pieces, you can totally use those in your reception space! If they differ from your centerpieces, use them as extra decor on the head table to set it apart.
- **What is your cancellation policy?** If ever you decide that the designer you choose isn't working out, or for some reason you need to move your wedding date, you'll want to know that you're not going to be on the hook for a ton of money.
- **Who do you recommend for linens/chairs/tableware?** Your florist will have tons of experience working with rental

companies, and whomever they recommend will probably be your best bet to book.

The DJ or Band

Any DJ or musician should allow you to come check out what they sound like at another wedding before booking them. Listen not only to the type of music they play but how their equipment, such as microphones and subwoofers, sound. Also check out if they're able to keep the energy up, the dance floor packed, and how their voice sounds on the mic.

When meeting with a DJ or musician, it's essential that you find out whether or not they play the clean or unedited version of songs (either way is fine, you just want to be on the same page...and maybe save Back That Ass Up for after 10pm), whether or not you can put a stop to requests (requests are seriously terrible, they can totally kill the vibe of the party when someone requests a song that isn't danceable), and if you can give a list of songs that you want played (the answer to this should always be yes; it's your wedding, so listen to what you like! Duh.) Ask what his or her 'go to' songs are to get people on the dance floor.

Almost as important as the play list is the Do Not Play list. You can give a list of songs that you absolutely hate so that the DJ makes sure not to play those songs. You don't have to think of every song you don't like; think of songs that you hear often at weddings and popular songs of the moment that you don't want played that night.

To save money, some people opt to put their iPods on shuffle and just plug it in to the speaker. There's a few reasons you should try to avoid this: one, DJs/musicians let everyone know what's happening. You need someone announcing you and your wedding party, when it's time to cut the cake, and when you're about to toss the bouquet. Two, you need someone to read the energy of the dance floor and decide on upcoming songs dependent on what people are responding to. Three, your iPod songs may not be the best songs to dance to. If you must skip the DJ, make sure your venue has a speaker and microphone you can use, and make a wedding playlist full of songs that you want everyone to dance to that night.

Additional questions to ask:

What equipment from the venue will you need access to, if any? Will they need a microphone? Subwoofers? Extension cords?

Do you provide uplighting, and what is the charge for that? Uplights are the small lights placed all around a room on the floor that face upward. They can completely transform the look of your space. I highly recommend going for it, and be sure you're able to select the colors and get a number of how many lights will be used. If they do provide uplighting, they should look at the space ahead of time to see how many they will need.

What's the backup plan if you can't make it due to an emergency?

What do you wear?

How many hours does my contract get me, and what if I want you to stay longer?

Do you provide music for cocktail hour?

Your DJ/band should ask you what specific songs you want played during certain times of the night. You should have songs chosen for your first dance, father/daughter dance, mother/son dance (if you decide to do this), cake cutting, bouquet toss and garter toss (if you do these). You should also pick the final song of the night.

I'm not a huge fan of coordinated dances, but those songs always get people on the dance floor. Two to three dances, such as the cha-cha slide and the hustle, make for a good time, but don't go overboard with every single coordinated dance known to mankind. And for the love of God, please don't do the chicken dance.

The Videographer

Videographers can be pricy, but in my opinion, it's worth the money to have a full account of everything that happened at your wedding. It's the only way to see the wedding how everyone else saw it!

Before booking a videographer, ask about their personal video style, and don't book them without seeing some of their work. Be sure to ask if the price includes editing, and how much of the wedding they film. (Do they film each of you getting ready beforehand? What about cutting the cake and tossing the bouquet at the reception?) How long will the video be once the editing is finished? When will the video be ready? Will you be able to ask for different edits after you see it, and will there be an additional charge for that? Side note: if they're not a large studio with multiple videographers, they should only be booking one wedding per day.

The Officiant

If you're getting married in a church or synagogue, you probably won't have a say in who marries you, but if you don't belong to a church and are looking to join one, spend some time with the priest/pastor/reverend and see who you connect well with.

If you're having a wedding outside of a church or synagogue, you'll need to find an officiant. For some reason, it was really tough finding one for our wedding. One creepy weirdo kept saying "hiiiii" over and over every time I tried to ask a question, and another time we got stood up by a lady who made us drive 40 minutes to meet with her.

Here's a list of questions you should ask in an email before meeting. Be sure that they answer all of your questions; this will be a test to see how well they pay attention.

Are you available on my wedding date?

What is your fee?

How many weddings do you do in a day?

Are you available for a dress rehearsal, and is there an additional fee for that?

Do you write the ceremony for us specifically, or do you use standard wording?

Can you send me some sample ceremony wording you've written?

Can we write our own vows? (This is also an important question to ask if you're getting married in a religious space.)

Do you perform non-denominational, interfaith or same-sex ceremonies? (If this applies to you.)

Once you find someone who answers all of your questions and seems to be a good match, you and your fiancé should meet with them to get a feel for their vibe and personality. Some of them will ask you to fill out a worksheet about you and your future spouse so that they can get an idea of who you are as a couple.

Ultimately, you should choose someone you like who seems to be confident enough to speak publicly and who is a talented ceremony writer. Be sure to also ask if you have any control over editing out things that you don't like from the ceremony.

Many people are now asking friends and loved ones to become ordained and perform their ceremonies. This can be a really cool option, but be sure that they know how the marriage license is supposed to be filled out and where they have to mail it to, and that they are a good enough writer to give you the ceremony experience that you're looking for.

Transportation

For the day of your wedding, you'll need to book some type of transportation. Even if you drive yourself to the ceremony and your wedding and reception are in the same place, you'll need to book transportation if you go offsite for photos. As an added bonus, the ride in the limo or party bus with your wedding party is so much fun and gives you extra time to spend with them before you're swarmed with the rest of your wedding guests.

Book your transportation in person so that you can see for yourself what their vehicles look like. It will also put your mind at ease to know that you've talked to someone in person. You should sign a contract with the transportation company just like every other vendor. It'll be a very simple contract, but it will hold them to something and you'll know they have in writing where and when your wedding is taking place. Ask if they provide anything special for weddings (such as champagne or specific music).

Transportation is usually paid by the hour (with some type of minimum amount of hours) and the prices will vary depending on where you go and what time of the year it is. Check your contract to see if gratuity is included in the price. If you're getting married during homecoming or prom season, you'll need to book way in advance. Whichever type of transportation you choose, be sure to account for you and your husband, your wedding party and your photographer so that there's enough room for everyone.

As far as after the reception goes, many hotels provide free shuttle service to nearby wedding locations, which is a great accommodation for your guests...especially those that go a little crazy with the drinks. Check with the hotel you decide to book a block of rooms with and see if they provide this service, how often the shuttle runs, and what time the shuttle service ends for the night. You can include this information in the accommodations section of your invitation.

10:

THE SKINNY ON BRIDAL SHOWS

One of my bridesmaids told me that I should go to one bridal show just to get the experience, and that it should be the big one because they are all the same type of deal. In Detroit, our largest bridal show is the Novi Bridal Expo.

A Bridal Expo is the same as most other expos…tons of vendor booths. If you are far along in the process of planning your wedding there isn't much to see unless you want to go with your girlfriends for fun. I will say, the food and cake samples made it worth my time.

When you first walk in, they have you fill out a card with your name, address, email and phone number. DO NOT WRITE YOUR REAL PHONE NUMBER. I never could have imagined the sheer volume of calls I would receive just from filling out that little sheet of paper. The individual vendors ask for your information when you visit them, so I only filled out my info at the booths I was interested in. I was under the impression that these booths were the only people who would be calling me because I had specifically expressed interest in their services. What they don't tell you is that the expo is sponsored by a number of vendors, and when you fill out your "registration form" in the front, the sponsors then get access to all of your information and will call you…and call you…and call you, for months after the show. Most of the places who call you are actually located at a call center out of state, so even if you do answer the call, you still have to make contact with whatever place they are calling on behalf of. It's a waste of time and it's annoying.

The part that I was most looking forward to at the expo was the fashion show. I *love* fashion and we got a spot in the front row so I was pretty excited. Bridal gowns and bridesmaid dresses were featured from one of the big box bridal stores. What a disaster. None of the models had been fitted properly. The dresses were all either skin tight, showing bulges on even the skinniest girls, or so loose that you could barely even tell what the shape of the dress was supposed to be. (It was really a testament to how important wedding dress alterations are.) One of the DJ vendors was the emcee for the show, which could have been a really great platform for him to gain business. Another disaster. Not only did he make the entire show about himself, but the sound system would cut in and out and constantly got feedback from the speakers, which he didn't even bother to try and fix. If anything, the bridal show may be a who's who of people *not* to use for your wedding.

I got something in the mail stating that during the second fashion show I won some type of skin rejuvenation service from a cosmetic surgery center which I, once again, had not given my information to. They do tons of giveaways but you might end up with something that you can't use.

You should go to one for the experience, but once you've seen one, there's no need to go to another, and if you value your sanity, you'll revert back to your single days and fake number that bitch.

11:
REGISTERING FOR GIFTS

Registering for gifts is SO FUN. It was definitely my favorite part of the wedding preparations. When my husband and I registered at Macy's, there was a lot of "What is that? WE NEED IT." We kept each other in check, though, and didn't put anything on the registry that we wouldn't use. Your registry gets auto imported into the store website so you can go back and change things if you need to update quantities, decide you don't want something, or you accidentally register for something when your fiancé "sees what happens" when you press the button from far away. Make an appointment on a weekday so that the store won't be crowded and you don't feel rushed. It took us about two hours to complete.

Two registries are fine, but anything more than that is obnoxious. You can choose places such as Amazon.com, which has practically everything, or The Home Depot for larger home items. FYI, registering online sucks. It's not that fun and it takes forever to go through everything.

When selecting items, be sure to hit all price points: under $50, $50-$75, $75-$100, and $100+ with several items to choose from in each category. As for the number of items you should register for, take your number of invited guests and then double it. You'll need to allow for multiple small gifts from one person, and enough for people to purchase something for both your shower and your wedding.

A couple people asked if we were going to register at all since we lived together for several years before our engagement and "already have everything." Um, that's a little presumptuous. Our dining sets were a hodge podge, our pans were all warped on the bottom, and there were a few items we didn't own at all. We also have completely different taste than we did so many years ago. We updated a couple of things along the way but there were still quite a few things that we needed. Don't let anyone make you feel bad for registering. You have just as much of a right to do so as everyone else, and it makes it easier on your guests so they know they're buying you something you actually want.

Don't reference your gift registry on your save-the-date or invitation. It's tacky and looks like you're angling for presents. Your bridesmaids should list your registry information on your bridal shower invitation.

You'll probably start to get gifts mailed to your house before your wedding from people who can't make it, so be sure to keep track from the first gift that arrives.

12:

SHOPPING FOR YOUR WEDDING DRESS

If you liked trying dresses on for prom, then you'll **love** shopping for a wedding gown. They're like prom dresses on steroids (both the dresses and the price tags.) You should set aside about 10% of your wedding budget for the dress.

Gowns take about six months to come in after ordering and you need time for alterations, which is why you need to start shopping for a dress at least eight months before your wedding.

Let's go over some basics for trying on bridal gowns:

- Choose a boutique bridal salon. I've heard horror stories about big box stores and even experienced some myself when I've been a bridesmaid. You'll get way more attention at a boutique and less errors tend to be made.
- Check which salons carry your favorite designers. You should be able to search the designer's website for locations near you.
- Only make appointments at salons that you have researched first. You have to be able to trust a boutique that will place your correct order when they are supposed to. Call to ask about price ranges so you know if it's the type of salon where you are able to buy.
- Don't go to a salon without an appointment. You won't get full attention and they'll probably be annoyed. Appointments usually last at least an hour.

- Wear a strapless bra and clothes that you can change in and out of easily.
- Be well rested. Some of the gowns were hard to get into and you have to be able to wrestle around and walk wearing 10lbs of fabric. One of the dresses I tried on I had to wear two skirts underneath to get the look I wanted and I was sweating my ass off.
- Don't go to more than 2 salons in a day. I was exhausted and ready for a nappy by the time I was done trying the dresses on.
- Keep an open mind. Just because you want a mermaid gown going in doesn't mean that's the kind of dress you HAVE to buy. I recommend trying a couple different styles just to get a feel for what looks good on your body.
- Keep your location in mind. Your dress should "go" with your venue.
- If you're ever feeling like you want something changed about a dress, ask your consultant if that particular designer allows it. Sometimes you can change a skirt or add or take away a sleeve. It doesn't hurt to ask!
- Try on the dresses your family wants you to try on. You don't have to buy one that they like but if you don't at least try it on they won't let it go. My mom really wanted me to try on a ball gown with a corset top with boning, which I knew I would never wear. After going back and forth with her I tried it on and I was right…I didn't like it. However, as soon as she saw that I wasn't into it after trying it on, she was able to let it go very easily.
- Take photos of top contenders if the salon allows you to do so. (Once you buy a dress, you will for sure be allowed to take a photo of

it.) Sometimes the consultant can do it for you in the room but not out in the open, so ask while you are in the room. Having photos to reference will keep your mind fresh about what the gowns look like. Besides, as Cher Horowitz said, always take photos, because you cannot trust mirrors.

- Don't try on dresses you can't afford. Stick to your budget. Even though it might be fun at first to try on top of the line gowns, you're setting yourself up for disappointment when the dresses you can afford don't compare.
- Don't buy a gown that day unless you are 100% sure that it's the one. Some salons offer you discounts if you order your dress that day, but don't do it just to get the bargain. I like to sleep on things before committing because you may feel differently once the initial excitement wears off.
- Bridal gowns tend to run small. It's bullshit and makes you feel bigger than you are (because that's what every bride needs...), so just know going in that you may have to buy a gown that is 1-2 sizes bigger than the size you normally wear. It's not just you, it's everyone.
- Limit the amount of people you bring to your appointments. For me, three was the perfect number. Everyone has different style and taste and you don't want so much outside influence that you get persuaded into a gown that you don't really want. Likewise, if you love something, you want people with you who will recognize that and support you regardless of whatever their personal opinion may be.
- You can wear white, no matter what. Or blush, or ivory, or whatever color looks good on your

skin type. Wear what you want to wear. Old school rules are for the birds.

It really does make a difference when you try a veil on. It was the first time that I looked at myself as an actual bride.

I tried three bridal salons and I tried on about 10 dresses at each place. It's a little easier being in your underwear in a room with a consultant you feel comfortable with, so if you're not feeling your person, ask for someone else. The only thing I thought was crazy was that one consultant didn't know what I was talking about when I referenced SJP's Vivienne Westwood gown in the Sex & The City movie!! WHAAAATTTTT.

The dress that I ended up buying was the first dress that I tried on at that salon, which seems to be the case for most brides. After I looked through all of the dresses in the store and decided that I wanted to try on the original dress for the second time, the owner brought over earrings, a necklace, and a veil, dimmed the lights, and I came out of the room in full garb. Everyone started crying which I wasn't expecting. Now, when I see consultants putting brides into veils and jewelry, I didn't think I liked that because I feel like sometimes they are playing on everyone's emotions by showing the bride what she will look like on her actual wedding day and when she has an emotional reaction it will make her more likely to buy the dress. However, it was nice to see how everything looked pulled together, and it ended up creating a very special moment for me and my family. Just be sure you're not buying into the *idea* of the look rather than the dress itself.

I wasn't into paying over $400 for a veil, so I ended up buying one at a trunk show. Trunk shows at bridal salons are events where discounts are offered on certain gowns and/or accessories, such as veils, tiaras, headbands, and jewelry. (Technically, there is also supposed to be a representative for the brand available to call it a "trunk show", but many salons just bring out a bunch of accessories at a discount and call it a trunk show.)

When budgeting for your dress, you must remember to allow room for alterations. Don't try to get around alterations. Having it tailored to your body is part of what makes wedding dresses look so amazing. Your first fitting should be about six weeks before the wedding, and you should be wearing your wedding shoes to get proper length alterations. When my dress came in and I had my first fitting, the bridal salon laid a ghastly alterations charge on me. $695, and all I needed was for it to be let out in the chest! I guess that's why they wouldn't give me any kind of estimate the day I ordered my dress. If they won't give you an idea of how much it's going to be, get to steppin' and find a new place; there's no rule that you have to get alterations at the same place you bought your dress. Check with your married friends to see who they used in instances such as these; you don't want to trust your alterations to a bad seamstress because they can fuck up the entire dress. My dress grazed the floor at my fitting and my seamstress decided not to take anything off the bottom, and I almost tripped over it and fell on my face as I was walking up the riser stairs to get married.

Be mindful when you look at gowns that you will need to also be purchasing undergarments depending on your dress type, such as a slip for a fitted silk dress or a hoop skirt to give a ball gown extra volume. Also take into consideration the retail tax, which can really add up for such a pricy purchase. Sixty percent of the price of the gown is usually due at the time of purchase before the salon will place your order. If you decide to purchase a gown off the rack, you'll have to pay the entire purchase price (but it's usually cheaper due to different fabric and beading than ordered gowns. Just make certain there aren't any stains/loose threads/that it's not so big that when you get it tailored it loses the silhouette entirely.)

There *is* such a thing as overshopping. If you try on too many gowns you will never be able to decide, and when you do purchase one you will be left wondering if you made the right decision. When you find a dress you love, stop looking.

Guys have it much easier. Joey and his groomsmen all went to a big box store to pick out the wedding tuxedos. They made a day of it and after the tuxes were chosen went out to eat and then out for wine and cigars while I was at home painting the kitchen like some kind of chump.

I ask a lot of questions. I need to know the 5 Ws & H, and when it came to my wedding, if I didn't get the answers I was looking for I immediately freaked out.

Me: "What day are the tuxes due back?"

Joey: "He didn't tell me."

Me: "Why is the pick up the Thursday before the wedding? That's not enough time if they fuck something up."

Joey: "That's just what he wrote down."

Me: "He wrote the pick-up for November, not October."

Joey: "Oh…well he said October."

Me: "Why are measurements due in June? That's too early."

Joey: "He said you could get remeasured."

Me: "Until when?"

Joey: "Not sure."

Therein lies the major difference between men and women. I have to know everything about everything and he's cool with the information someone offers. Obviously I immediately made plans to go to the store myself and straighten this all out. I got the pick-up moved up a day and the drop off got moved one day later because they had them due back the day after the wedding, and I also had them put a note to allow measurements through August. It was crazy busy in there because it was both wedding and prom season; when you're discussing your wedding arrangements, you HAVE to make your voice heard. They talk over you and half listen so you need to make sure you're getting exactly what you want.

13:

STATIONERY

Save-the-Dates

You'd be surprised how hard it is to find a modern design for Save-the-Dates. Every site I went to had the same boring designs. (Head over to TheRealistBride.com and choose stationery by your wedding theme to find options I've hand-selected.) I am a perfectionist so I spent more than a few hours doing "mock ups" of ours. Also I felt important saying that I was doing "mock ups."

Your Save-the-Dates should have your exact wedding date and location, so don't send them until you've booked your venue. You don't have to get crazy with the details just yet. All that matters is that you've announced you're getting married and where and when it's happening.

I thought I wanted to hand print names on our Save-the-Dates envelopes, and my mom thought they should be in cursive. According to Joey, "cursive is dead." We each addressed one and hers looked way better, so we did them all in cursive. Maybe once in a while Mom does know best. Put the person with the worst handwriting in charge of stuffing and stamping envelopes.

Invitations

Have you ever spent 20 minutes searching for the perfect "J" font? Welcome to hell, or as it's better known, invitation shopping. I was unaware that there could even *be* drama regarding paper products, but I was wrong.

I had been eyeballing an invitation website since before I was engaged. I loved the modern style. Joey and I met with the owner. I asked to see some samples of invitations and she kind of shocked me when she only brought a couple of invitations with her because the invitations are completely custom...but how can you make a decision without looking at all of the options? It's not the bride's job to come up with a concept...that's the whole point of going custom made.

I loved the work that I had seen thus far and so we decided to book her after she provided us with a quote. I mailed her our deposit check.

A couple days later, she emailed me saying that the color I had chosen for our RSVP envelope was not available and apologized for the oversight. I was a little annoyed but changed the color and moved on.

A couple of days after that, she sent me another email stating that the invitation envelopes didn't come in the color that I wanted either. I was pretty furious at that point. I happen to think that if you are paying the extra price for custom invitations that you should be able to get whatever effing color you want. I called Joey to bitch about it and he told me to ask her if she could order the envelope custom to the color that we wanted from her wholesaler. She found out that she could and emailed me the custom upcharge.

Her third email, which was the last straw, was a list of the colors that I wanted...and the color was wrong. I thought about it and realized that I just could not trust her to get the invitations right.

I emailed her and stated all of the problems, and that she should mail me my deposit back. She responded by saying that I was totally right and that she was "incompetent with this project." It's important to trust your gut. If something feels wrong, there's a reason.

Thankfully we ended up finding a professional brick and mortar store that gave us beautiful invitations. If you do decide to go custom, expect guidance with your invitations, but they'll want a general idea from you of how you want everything worded. There's also ways you can save money by going custom; we had them print everything, including labels and adhering them to the envelopes, but you can put the actual invitation itself together to save a little money. There should be an itemized quote sheet that you can go off of to decide what you do and don't want.

Here's a guide to getting started with your invitations:

- **Decide which type of invitation you want.** Do you want a simple one piece invite plus RSVP card? What about a pocketfold invitation? How about a passport invitation for a destination wedding? Are you printing them yourself, or are you going custom?
- **Choose your card stock**. Go for something thick that has a little weight to it, and if you're into sparkle, pick something with sheen. It makes the invitation look very expensive.

- **Decide on your font.** It sounds like a silly thing to worry about, but your font can represent the vibe of the wedding you'll have...casual, whimsical, romantic, or grand?
- **Decide if you're printing labels, hiring a calligrapher, or hand addressing them.**

For labels: Do a test print on your computer to make sure your printer can accommodate what you want to do, and that the ink doesn't smear.

For calligraphy: Calligraphy is the art of producing decorative handwriting or lettering with a pen or brush. Each calligrapher has a different style, so check out their previous work and be sure they have positive reviews. Calligraphers tend to charge between $2-$5 per envelope.

For hand addressing: Invest in a few good pens, start doing wrist exercises, and start early, because it's going to take a while.

Once your invitations come in and it's time to start putting them together:

- **Enlist your parents and/or bridesmaids to help you stuff your invitations.** We opted for pocketfold invites and it was really helpful to have a number of people to create an assembly line putting them together.
- **Use glue sticks instead of licking envelopes.** It's faster and won't gross you

out...plus, I think we've all seen what happened to George Costanza's fiancée Susan.

- **Don't forget to put stamps on the RSVP cards.** The inner envelopes for RSVP cards should have a stamp in the top right corner so that your guests don't have to worry about a stamp to send in their RSVP.
- **Weigh your invitations before sending them.** This is a big one! A regular stamp is not going to be enough postage! Bring one fully completed invitation to the post office and ask them to weigh it; they'll give you a total price of postage needed. They usually have a larger piece of postage in a wedding theme available, but depending on the invite, you may need a large *and* a small piece of postage on each invitation.
- **Mail your invites beginning 3 months before the big day.** It gives enough time to remind them of the date without being so far in advance that they forget to RSVP.
- **Send your invitations in batches.** Staggering them will help avoid getting a ton at once (although you will almost certainly get a bunch right around the RSVP due date.) This also helps if you have some people in your "maybe" pile; you can send them out as regrets come in. Start with immediate family, bridal party, and out-of-town guests.
- **Ask the post office to hand cancel them.** Canceling is the term the post office uses for

marking stamps on mail from being re-used. The post office puts mail through a machine to automatically do this, but this can tear or mark up your invitations. If you drop your invitations off in person, you can ask the desk clerk to have them hand canceled so that they don't get put through the machine. They didn't charge me to do it, but I've heard of some places trying to charge you. If they do, try asking a different post office near you.

- As soon as you mail the first batch, **keep track on your guest list spreadsheet**, marking who has responded, which meal they selected (if you're having a plated meal), and how many guests are coming from their invitation.

Wedding Invitation Etiquette & Wording

There is a method to how wedding invitations should be worded. Here's an overview.

The names of the hosts should be listed at the top of the invitation. (The hosts of the wedding are the people who are paying for it.)
The invitation should include:
- Ceremony day of week, date and time
- Location with address
- Dates, times, streets and states spelled out
- Zip codes are not used on invitations themselves, but can be included on accommodation or direction cards

The phrase "request the honor of your presence" is usually used in more formal ceremonies or if the wedding will be held at any house of worship. If your ceremony is more casual, "request your presence at their marriage", or "joyfully invite you to their wedding celebration" are options, but you can come up with your own way to say it, too. Choose whatever sounds best to you and your fiancé.

Wording Examples

Parents of the bride are paying and the wedding is at their house:

Mr. and Mrs. Kenneth Williams
request the pleasure of your company
at the marriage of their daughter
Jessica Lynn Williams
to
Joseph Michael Gomez
Saturday, the eleventh of October
two thousand and fourteen
at half-past five o'clock in the evening
789 Grand Avenue
Livonia, Michigan

Both sets of parents are paying:

Mr. and Mrs. Kenneth Williams
And Mr. and Mrs. Sydney Gomez
request the honor of your presence
at the marriage of their children
Jessica Lynn Williams
to
Joseph Michael Gomez
Saturday, the eleventh of October
two thousand and eighteen
at half-past five o'clock in the evening

Saint Colette Catholic Church
1234 Harrison Boulevard
Canton, Michigan

Bride and groom are paying for some or most and parents/other family members are contributing:

Together with their families
Jessica Lynn Williams
&
Joseph Michael Gomez
request the pleasure of your company
at the celebration of their marriage
Saturday, the eleventh of October
two thousand and nineteen
at five o'clock in the evening
The Hilltop Country Club
456 Main Street
Detroit, Michigan

Bride and groom are paying for everything:

Jessica Lynn Williams
&
Joseph Michael Gomez
request the honor of your presence
as they are joined together in marriage
Saturday, the eleventh of October
two thousand and twenty
at five o'clock in the evening
The Grand Ballroom at The MGM Grand
123 Main Street
Detroit, Michigan

Divorced parents of the groom are paying:

Ms. Regina Gomez
Mr. Simon Gomez
request the honor of your presence
at the marriage of their son
Joseph Michael Gomez
to
Jessica Lynn Williams
Saturday, October 11th
two thousand and sixteen
at half-past five o'clock in the evening
The Grand Ballroom at The MGM Grand
123 Main Street
Detroit, Michigan

Divorced parents of the bride are paying and one parent has remarried:

Ms. Joanna Smith
Mr. and Mrs. Kenneth Williams
request the honor of your presence
at the marriage of their daughter
Jessica Lynn Williams
to
Joseph Michael Gomez
Saturday, the twenty-third of June
two thousand and seventeen
at half-past five o'clock
Temple Beth El
567 Plymouth Road
Detroit, Michigan

Reception Cards

Reception card wording is pretty self explanatory; you list the reception site, time, and address.

Reception Card Wording Examples

The celebration continues at a dinner reception
immediately following the ceremony
The Angelica Ballroom
333 Main Street
Canton, Michigan

Eat. Drink. Dance.
at seven o'clock in the evening
The Williams Hotel
Ballroom C
555 Grand River Avenue
Farmington Hills, Michigan

Reception
immediately following the ceremony
at the residence of
Mr. and Mrs. Kenneth Williams
888 Five Mile Road
Livonia, Michigan

If the ceremony and reception are being hosted in the
same location, there is no need for a reception card;
just be sure to include "Reception immediately
following" or "Cocktails and hors d'oeuvres
immediately following. Dinner served at seven
o'clock" at the bottom of the invitation.

Response Cards

Response cards are what your guests use to RSVP,
and they usually start with a line with an M, indicating
where the guest should write their name. (M is for Mr.,
Ms. or Mrs.) It's not necessary, though. Choose
whichever way you prefer.

RSVP Card Wording Examples

The favor of a reply is requested by September twenty-second

Name(s) _____

_____ will attend

_____ will not attend

Or:

M_____

_____ Accepts with pleasure

_____ Declines with regret

In the bottom left corner: Kindly respond by September 22.

Entrée

____Poultry

____Fish

____Vegetarian

Only list meals on the card if you're having a plated meal; it's irrelevant for a buffet. (You can get more specific here and describe each meal, especially if it adheres to a certain dietary requirement, such as gluten-free or vegan.)

You can get creative with the attending/not attending wording options, especially if you're having a casual ceremony, such as "Can't Wait!" or "I'll be there in spirit."

Give yourself a buffer of two weeks before the final tallies are actually due to allow for people who don't RSVP on time.

Accommodations Card

The accommodations card should have the name, address, and contact information for the hotel where you've blocked rooms, as well as the name it is blocked under. Include any necessary parking information, such as complimentary valet or a nearby parking structure, and if there's a shuttle from the ceremony to reception or reception to the hotel.

If you're having a destination wedding, you should include other pertinent information on this card, such as car rental companies or nearby attractions.

Directions Card

The directions card should include the name and address of your ceremony and your reception locations. Spelled out directions should be included from all major freeways to your ceremony, and then spelled out directions from your ceremony to your reception should also be included. You can also include a map if you'd like, but it's not as necessary anymore since most people have smart phones with GPS.

If you have enough space on the card, you can save extra money by putting your accommodations and directions on the same card.

Inner Envelope Addressing

The small, inner envelope is used for RSVP return cards. Your name (however you want it: 'Jessica Williams and Joseph Gomez' or 'The Williams-Gomez Wedding' both work) and address should be printed on the front as they will be mailing their RSVP to your home.

Outer Envelope Addressing

Names and streets should be spelled out completely. (Benjamin rather than Ben, Kathleen rather than Kathy; circle, lane rather than Cir or Ln.)

Use names, not "guest." You should only use "and guest" if you have no idea who the invited is bringing. Before my husband and I were married, we were invited to his cousin's wedding. We had been living together for a few years and I had met his cousin several times. The invitation had his name and a guest. It was incredibly insulting...I was the one who grabbed it from our mailbox!

The word "and" in between two names implies that those guests are married. Names of unmarried hosts and guests should be on separate lines. Widows should be addressed as Mrs., not Ms.

Example of how to address married couple invitations:

Mr. and Mrs. Kenneth Williams
5678 Blank Avenue
Canton, Michigan 48187

Example of how to address unmarried guest
invitations:

Mr. John Smith
Ms. Georgia Johnson
1234 Sunny Street
Livonia, Michigan 48154

The return address should be printed or stamped on
the back flap of the outer envelope.

Fun Fact: You can send a wedding invitation to the
President, and the White House sends you a
personalized memento back congratulating you on
your wedding!

Escort Cards

Escort cards are the little cards that your guests will pick up from the table outside of your reception to see the table number at which they'll be seated. They also serve as a tool for your wait staff to see what meals your guests have selected if you're having a plated dinner. Some people choose to put a little picture of the food on the card, but I find it more elegant to place the first letter of the type of meal they'll have in the corner of the card. (For example, if your choices are Eggplant or Ravioli, you would place an E or an R in the corner of the card.) It doesn't matter what symbol you choose, just be sure to let your site coordinator and caterer know what it is so you're all on the same page.

Place cards are cards with each person's name that are placed on each table, giving assigned seating to each person. This is only necessary at extremely formal weddings. The only table I used place cards for was at the head table.

Don't go crazy spending money on escort cards. You can get very simple ones and jazz them up with a nice font. If you're a DIY kind of bride, these should be very simple to make. Printing directly on the card is much easier to read than hand writing them.

If you're having a buffet for dinner and people don't need to pre-select their meals, try a sign listing names and table numbers.

Speaking of which, you're going to need table numbers! Some venues have numbers and stands available, but ask to see what they look like, because if you aren't satisfied with them you'll need to add numbers and stands to your list of things to buy and drop off to the venue.

As far as menus go, they're completely for show because your menu is decided well in advance of the wedding. They're only used for formal weddings, and even then, not a necessity.

When it comes to ordering your wedding stationery, keep in mind that if you have 100 total guests and they're all couples, you'll only need 50 invitations. Always order at least 10% extra to allow for mistakes or last minute guest additions, and don't forget to set an extra aside for yourselves.

14:

PLANNING YOUR HONEYMOON

Since I did most (all) of the planning for our wedding, I let Joey choose the honeymoon spot, and he chose Italy. The lady who did our wedding invitations advised us not to go to Europe for our honeymoon because there is too much running around and you can't relax much. On the outside I said "thanks for the advice" and on the inside I said "mind your own business, biatch." AS IT TURNS OUT she was correct!

Neither of us had been out of the country, so we had to apply for passports. You'll need to schedule an appointment for this. I had typed most of the form ahead of time but filled in a couple of answers in pen that I didn't know the answers to when I was filling the form out online. I handed over the forms and the clerk said that it had to be in black ink, so I grabbed a black pen and re-wrote over the information. If you're handwriting your form, use black ink (even though I believe she may have made this rule up.) Be aware that when you apply for a passport, they take your original birth certificate and send it with your forms, and then mail it back to you with your passport. I recommend getting an extra copy of your birth certificate ahead of time just in case.

We considered using a travel agent to book our details but for some reason most agencies don't do European travel. If you know of anyone who has been to your destination, ask for their advice! They will most likely give you a tidbit you wouldn't have known without them.

The process of booking your details will be grueling. Finding an affordable flight without multiple stops or a long layover time is tough, but it is doable. If you're just booking a flight I would recommend going through the airline, but since we were doing a flight and hotel package it ended up being much cheaper through Expedia.

Isn't it annoying when you're looking online for the best things to do around the country and there are lists that say "watch the sunset" and "take a walk"? WOW I was not going to do those things until you told me, thank you for the helpful guide!

There are a million things to do if you honeymoon in a Western European country, which is a good thing and a bad thing. If you're looking for culture and history, it's a great choice. If you're looking to relax and take it easy...not so much. The walking alone is a feat.

The first stop on our honeymoon was Roma (Rome.) Why do we have English names for cities in other countries? Ridiculous. Speaking of language, nothing in Italy is in English...even at the airport and train stations. I recommend some Rosetta Stone time before visiting a country whose first language is not English. One time we bought a ticket to what we thought was a train but it actually was for a bus. Doesn't matter, we missed the bus.

Rome is a very interesting place. It has a bustling city life and then right beside it, and sometimes right in the middle of it, are ancient monuments. The first couple of days we took tours. The first day was a tour of the Colosseum and the Roman Forum, finishing on Palatine Hill. The next tour was of the Catacombs under the Appian Way, Basilica de San Clemente, and Capuchin Crypts. If you're into creepy stuff like this, it is a MUST DO. I caught myself smiling like a big weirdo when we were underground in the catacombs.

Outside the Colosseum

We noticed that although Italians pretty much all speak English, they aren't very interested in helping you... but unless you read Italian, you will need help at some point.. or in our case since we were traveling a lot, at many points. The only way I figured out how to get to Pompeii and Capri from where we were was through comments on TripAdvisor. (TripAdvisor is essential when traveling. Use it before you try to go anywhere you haven't been before.)

We visited the extremely crowded Vatican City. Heads up, don't bring a backpack if you're going to the museum. You have to go through security like at the airport and then they make you check all bags at the front, and they neglect to tell you that the only way to get your bag back is to go all the way around the entire Vatican property back where you started to get back to it, which is about a 20 minute brisk walk. One of the highlights of the trip was seeing Michelangelo's work at the Sistine Chapel inside the Vatican Museum. Photos were not permitted, which we found to be the rule at several churches.

Next, we took the Frecciarossa (smooth, high speed train) on a two hour trip to Firenze (Florence.)

Florence is much different from Rome. It's still full of shops but the city is smaller and it's surrounded by hills. Up in the hills it's SUPER quiet, and the view is unreal.

The Arno River in Florence

Finally, it was on to Venezia (Venice.) Joey walked to a nearby hotel to ask where to go and they advised us to take a local train and then a waterbus.

You have to just know which stop to get off at on the waterbus, which I only knew because I had once again looked it up on the comments of TripAdvisor. There was no way to tell which stop you were at without asking, so we technically could have been riding around on the boat for hours.

Once we got off at the stop (you have approximately three seconds before they continue on) we just looked at each other like "now what?" Venice closes down at about 10pm and by this time it was 11…no shops open, no restaurants open, nothing. There are no cars in Venice so you can't just tell a taxi driver to take you to your hotel. The streets in Venice are like alleyways that wind and turn and end without warning. We were alone, had no idea where we were, it was dark, at this point we were both sick, and we were more than a little frustrated. I yelled out into the night, my voice echoing "THIS IS UNBELIEVABLE!!!" An American woman, like an angel, appeared out of the darkness and asked if we needed help and told us where to go. Just as mysteriously as she arrived, she was gone. Joey "didn't trust her" but we ended up at our hotel.

We were shown to our hotel room…on the ground floor. Every time someone checked in or out or took the elevator, we could hear every word spoken. I was thoroughly annoyed by this, but not quite as annoyed as I was by the size of the bed…actually, the size of the room in general. It was constructed for elves. The bathroom door couldn't be opened all the way without moving our luggage onto the bed. The bed was tiny. I marched the five steps back to the front desk and said that we were supposed to have a King bed. He said "All of the beds are the same. They are all Kings." (They don't have King sized beds in Italy, but they put two mattresses together to make it a King, as I learned at my two previous hotels. This bed had one mattress that was no larger than a twin.) I just glared at him and retreated back to my closet.

It was freezing in the room. As I was pushing the thermostat, nothing was happening. When I pressed more forcefully, the unit fell into the wall. I decided to take a hot shower to warm up. Unfortunately the shower had no tub and was flush with the floor, so when I turned the water on, first it sprayed all over the toilet and toilet paper, then all over the entire floor of the bathroom. Joey said all he could hear was me in the bathroom yelling "WHAT THE FUCK" and "GOD DAMN IT."

Once we got out of the hotel and into the light of day, we saw that Venice is beautiful and very unique, and in my opinion, they had the best shopping out of all of the places we visited.

On a gondola ride

It was almost double the plane ticket price to depart out of Venice, so we traveled back to Rome by train for three and a half hours. When we checked in to our final hotel we learned from a flyer that it was daylight savings time (not the same day as in America) to add a little extra stress to the day.

When we got dropped off at our terminal at 4:30am, the door to the airport didn't open. We looked inside and saw no one and immediately knew something was wrong. We pulled out our itinerary and in tiny letters under Delta it said "Operated by Air France." We asked a rogue worker where the Air France terminal was and were told it was "far." So we started hoofing it within the airport property outside. Thankfully a random taxi was driving by, so we hopped the fence and flagged him down.

When we landed in France for our layover we had to figure out how to get our boarding passes to the US because for some reason our layover passes had not printed at the kiosk in Italy. Once we got them, we made our way to the gate where it said "Last Call for Boarding." We were thoroughly confused. We boarded and the pilot came over the speaker apologizing for the "20 minute delay to change a tire." OHHHH apparently France does not have daylight savings that day, and our layover was 30 minutes...NOT an hour and 30 minutes. If there hadn't been a delay, we would have missed our plane home. So, I guess check for daylight savings time in every country you'll be stopping in!

We had a good time on the trip but there were a lot of stressful moments. I guess there's a reason most people go to Hawaii for their honeymoon.

When planning your honeymoon, here's some tips on how to get the most out of your experience:

- Leave on a weekday. Midweek plane tickets and hotel rooms are cheaper than weekends.

- Tell everyone you're booking with that you're on your honeymoon because most places will give you something. For us, it was a room upgrade in Rome and a bottle of wine in Florence.
- Research the best/most romantic/best view restaurants and keep the information with you on your trip so you don't end up eating at random places every meal. If you're heading to a touristy place, you're going to get some touristy (read: bad) restaurants, and the research you do in advance will ensure you have at least one amazing meal. Ask your hotel concierge for their recommendations as well. Avoid restaurants that have photos of food because their aim is trapping tourists, not providing great meals to locals.
- Visit Viator.com to book any day trips or visits to places your honeymoon spot is known for. Many of the popular monuments have insanely long lines, and Viator has tons of "skip the line" options. We used City Wonders for our tours through Viator and they were fantastic.
- Make sure your phone works where you're going. If you don't travel a lot, odds are, you don't have an international phone plan. Do not leave this to chance and get a thousand dollar phone bill. Call your phone provider and give them the dates you'll be out of the country and pay the extra fee for one month of an international plan. Side note: some American places also need this plan. Our phones worked when we visited St. Thomas, but in St. John, they immediately started roaming.

- Check CDC.gov to see if you need any vaccinations before traveling to your destination.
- Research the cultural tipping norm for the place you're headed. Many countries don't customarily tip, or may tip much less than you're used to, so you could save yourself some major cash.
- Check to see if you'll need a special adapter for the country you'll be traveling to. Most countries don't use the same kind of plugs that we have, and if you try to plug in your hair dryer, phone, etc. with an American charger, it'll short everything out.
- Let your bank and credit cards know in advance when you'll be out of town. The last thing you want is to be stuck in another country with no money because your bank thinks your card has been stolen.
- Change your currency at your bank before you leave if you're not traveling to an American territory. We forgot to do this ahead of time and we paid dearly for it.

If you're planning on traveling to Europe for your honeymoon, here are some additional tips:

- Beware of pick pockets. In Italy, they were the most prevalent in city meccas, but they are really everywhere. They'll cut your purse off of your shoulder so cross bodies aren't a great idea. Everyone wears their backpacks in the front to avoid them. If I wasn't so repulsed by fanny packs it would have been the perfect solution. Thankfully I had been made aware of the pick pocket situation so I held my purse close like a newborn baby if I carried one at all. Don't carry a ton of cash or your passports if you don't need them, and obviously only use front pockets.

- Cover up when visiting ancient churches. Some of them require you to have your shoulders and legs covered. You can check online to see what the rules are for individual churches but it's better to err on the side of caution.
- Map out where you want to go and research how to get there ahead of time. Most people don't want to help you, so you have to be as self sufficient as possible. Our google maps randomly stopped working overseas, so don't rely on your phone. Use TripAdvisor as much as possible while you've got reliable wi-fi at your hotel.
- There are street peddlers everywhere. Don't be afraid to firmly say "no." Please do not buy a selfie stick.
- Eat what the region is known for. In Italy, it's wine, cheese and gelato. My GOD, the gelato. If you're not a wine connoisseur but want to dabble in what the region has to offer, try asking for the house wine; it's usually a good and reasonably priced option.
- PACK LIGHT. I cannot stress this enough. You will be walking a ton, you'll be doing stairs, and if you're planning on taking the train between cities there's really only room for one bag per person.
- Be ready to spend a lot of money. Pretty much everything in Europe costs money, including toilets and water…and some places have a cover charge just for eating there.

Wherever you decide to go, leave some time to relax. You'll be coming off of a very stressful time, so enjoy your vacation with your new spouse as much as you can.

15:

THE BRIDAL SHOWER

Bridal showers are traditionally thrown by bridesmaids, but sometimes brides have two showers because someone at work wants to throw them one, or both sides of the family are so large that someone on your fiancé's side hosts one as well. As long as the bride or bride's parents aren't throwing the shower, this is totally acceptable. (Parents throwing your shower is considered poor taste because it's seen as your family asking for gifts.)

When making your bridal shower guest list, remember that everyone invited to the shower must also be invited to the wedding. However, you don't have to invite every female who is invited to your wedding. In fact, I'm sure your bridesmaids would appreciate you NOT inviting everyone.

Make sure that your friends, your close family and your husband's close family are invited. That great aunt that you haven't seen in years? It's not necessary to invite them. If you have out-of-town guests that you're close with, send them an invitation even if you know they can't make it. It'll make them feel included.

Leave it up to your future husband if he wants to attend the shower or not. Normally the guy comes at the end to load up the gifts and say hi really quick, but mine "didn't want to miss out on the food", so he was there for the whole thing. I also invited my dad, because I knew he would like to be there for it. It's up to you to decide if the main men will be there or not.

If you want to do a co-ed shower, also known as a Jack and Jill shower, that's your prerogative. I'll let you in on a little secret, though: guys don't care about bridal showers. If you're going to do a co-ed, you'll need to have a different type of shower. Keep it casual and fun. Ask your bridesmaids if they're up for something unique, such as hosting at a vineyard with wine tasting, having a barbeque, or at the very least, including games that men will enjoy as much as women. Just be mindful of the guest list because you don't want to leave too hefty of a price tag to your bridal party, and including men will double the list. A final tip for co-ed showers: alcohol is a must.

Because I am a busy body control freak I knew a lot about my bridal shower beforehand. Unless your shower is a surprise, you should be allowed to give heavy hints about what color scheme you like and if you have a specific theme in mind. My bridesmaids came up with a list of places to throw it and I visited a few options with my MOH and ultimately decided on the place. The bridesmaids had great ideas of places to host it but some places never responded, some places were rude, and others outrageously expensive, so be prepared for that.

My bridesmaids set up a "something old, something new, something borrowed, something blue" theme which was a surprise and it was such a cute idea. For "something borrowed", they passed around a notebook where everyone could write advice for us as newlyweds. It ended up being one of my favorite things from the shower.

Nail polish favors with heart cut outs. Thanks
Pinterest!

Everyone should be fed at your shower in some way.
If someone is having it at their house, a multitude of
snacks or appetizers and beverages should be
available. These people are coming to your shower to

give you presents, so the least they can get back is some food!

Something old...photos of us. Homecoming and prom photos included!

Be sure to spend a little time with every person that attends your shower. Thank each guest for coming on the way in and on the way out.

One thing no one mentions about the shower...your house will become a disaster area when you bring all your loot home. I should have made room beforehand, but the gifts took up our entire kitchen. We had four full loads of dishes of JUST new items. It took several days to get everything put away and organized. I had to completely rearrange our kitchen in order to make everything fit.

Do your thank you notes right away. You'll have one less thing to think about, and you **must** get all shower thank you notes out before the wedding.

16:

TRADITIONS & TRENDS YOU CAN SKIP

Make your life easier and your expenses smaller by skipping these money sucking traditions and trends.

Photo Booth: Photo booths at weddings are extremely popular right now. While their presence at weddings isn't bothersome, I've heard "the photo booth was the best part of the wedding!" one too many times...if someone said that about my event I would have a meltdown. You want everyone on the dance floor and socializing with each other, not waiting in line to take "funny" photos that you now see at almost every wedding. Trust me, your photographer will catch all the photos you need, so skip the added expense. If you're dead set on it, go for a Video Booth instead, where guests can record their well wishes and even answer questions that you pre-select for them.

Multiple Wedding Dresses: I understand the concept behind them when you want a dress that you can easily dance in, but you (hopefully) only get married once...don't you want to bask in the glory of the big white dress for one full day? Not to mention, it takes time away from your guests when you change, and it could possibly ruin your hair and makeup.

Programs: Do you really need to read along at a wedding? I think we all get the gist.

Guest Book: The guest book is more about tradition than utility. You already have everyone's

information- you're the one who sent them invitations!

Favors: We didn't do them, and no one missed them. Unless you're doing something deeply personal or they're integral to your wedding theme, it's okay to forego the favors.

Groom's Cake: Trust me, I love cake, and trust me again when I say that one is enough.

Flower Girl & Ring Bearer: I had them, but that doesn't mean you have to. You can save yourself from worrying about their attire, their gifts for being in the wedding, the flower basket and the ring pillow, and even save from making others mad that their kids weren't included.

The Veil: Veils are expensive, so if you're not into them, don't feel like you need to buy one! If you feel naked without a little something, try a sparkling headband or a hair pin. If a veil is a must, save by avoiding floor length veils and beading, which really jack up the price.

17:

OBTAINING YOUR MARRIAGE LICENSE

You should apply for a marriage license about four weeks before your wedding, but certificates are only good for a certain amount of time, so check with the clerk's office for the county in which you'll be married and check all of their guidelines. Ask how much it will cost (and what methods of payment are accepted), and whether or not they require a blood test. Here's what you'll need to bring with you to apply:

- Your fiancé
- Certified copies (should have raised seal) of both of your birth certificates
- Driver's Licenses (or any government issued photo IDs)
- Blood test results (if required in your state)
- If you've been divorced, divorce decree
- If you're a widow, death certificate of your former spouse

Pay for an extra official copy of the marriage license just in case.

The ceremony officiant will fill out the certificate on the day of your wedding once it's obtained. You'll both sign it right before or right after the ceremony, and the officiant will mail it in to be officially filed with the state. Double check with your officiant to be sure they've done it before and know where to send it. The clerk's office will send you a copy of your official marriage certificate within a couple of weeks. Treat it as you do your birth certificate and passport and file it away in a safe place.

18:
RSVP: FIND OUT WHAT IT MEANS TO ME

Any former bride can attest that RSVP time is one of the hardest parts of the wedding planning process. It is so rude not to RSVP to any kind of formal event, let alone a wedding. It's hard enough (and expensive enough!) getting the invitations out, and to not get a response is basically saying "I don't even like you enough to send you an RSVP." What I don't understand is why people can't bring themselves to drop the envelope in the mail. The postage is paid for, the envelope is addressed…all you have to do is fill out two little boxes, yet, I think you'd be hard-pressed to find a bride who hasn't had a problem with getting RSVPs back.

If you're having a plated meal at your wedding, RSVP cards are especially important because you have to give an exact number of each meal to your venue or caterer.

When RSVPs do start to come in, avoid being upset about the people who decline and realize how much money you're going to save! You can be pissed about people who RSVP yes and don't show, though. Those people are The Devil.

When my RSVP due date came, I was still missing about 50 cards. It is not your job to hunt every single person down; you have enough going on. All those people your parents just had to invite and now you haven't heard from them? Time to put your parents to work and get their people to send their RSVP cards in. As for your friends that haven't RSVPed, shoot them a text or email reminding them that you haven't received their RSVP yet and that you need to know if they're coming or not so you can give a final count to the caterer/venue. (This might be a good task to give to your fiancé.) If they don't respond, count them as a no. Odds are they aren't coming and don't want to say so, but on the off chance that they're just super rude and show up anyway, your venue or caterer should be able to make accommodations for that. You'll have to check your contract, but normally it will say something along the lines of being able to serve not more than 10% above the number of the final count. Plan on having a few guests who RSVP that they are coming and then don't show; medical and personal issues come up for some, and others are just dicks. Anyone who comes without RSVPing can have the meals of the people who don't show.

As for people who do RSVP...you're going to get a few people putting a plus one on their RSVP card who you weren't planning on giving one. Use your judgment for this; if you've gotten a bunch of regrets, it's better to avoid a stressful situation and just allow the person to bring the guest that they've RSVPed. If your budget is super tight, though, just explain that the venue has limitations and you couldn't even invite everyone you wanted to invite yourself, and that you're sorry but you aren't giving plus ones to anyone who isn't engaged or married.

19:

CREATING YOUR SEATING CHART

Some brides let guests pick their own spot for dinner, but I encourage you NOT to do this. It can make guests feel anxious and left out if their friends' table is filled up by the time they get there, forcing them to sit with a bunch of people they don't know. It's very high school, so avoid it altogether.

You'll want to go over the seating arrangements with your site coordinator before making your seating chart. You'll need to let them know if you're doing a sweetheart table (just you and your new spouse) or if you want your entire wedding party at the head table. (You don't have to put their spouses and kids at your table unless you want to.) Ask if they have round, square, or rectangular tables or if you can mix them, and how many people you can comfortably sit at each. Once you know which type of seating you want, ask them to put together a diagram of a couple different options so you can get an idea of what your reception set up will look like and so you'll know which table number corresponds with which tables. Once you've finalized your reception tables diagram, forward a copy to your florist so they can start to visualize the space.

I started out by buying a poster board and some tab post-its. The seating chart can't be made more than a couple weeks in advance because you need to know who is and isn't attending. For each guest who has confirmed that they are attending, write their name on a tab (use your spreadsheet for reference.) If you want to get really OCD with it, you can specify each color to mean something different. For example, orange tabs are your guests, and blue tabs are your parents' guests.

I printed out the diagram of our reception space and glued it to the poster board, then started putting people at each table. It's important to use post-its because even though you may think you have a pretty good idea of who is sitting where, there's a lot of moving parts. It's inevitable that people are going to have to be moved from table to table while figuring it out, and it's much easier to move the tab than to keep scribbling names out.

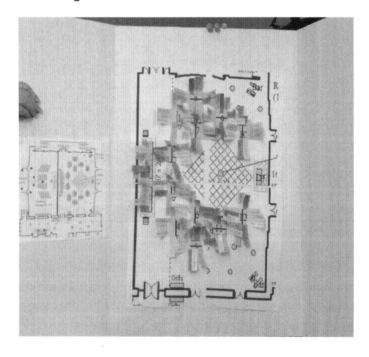

If you're unable to get a diagram of the space, use a protractor to draw even circles on your poster board.

Making the seating chart wasn't quite as fun as I hoped it would be. It's harder than it sounds. I invited our parents over to help because I figured they would have some insight as to who they think should sit with whom, which I recommend you do as well. Just be prepared to butt heads on some seating opinions.

When deciding which guests should sit where, you should put the bride's immediate family at the closest table to the head table, followed by the groom's immediate family. From there, it really doesn't matter which table numbers you give people, but you can opt to put the people you are least close to furthest from you. Try to seat people who know each other together so that everyone can see a familiar face. It's okay to have a kids table if you have enough kids to fill one, but try to avoid having a "singles" table because it might embarrass your guests. Don't drive yourself too insane over the seating chart, though. They're only going to be at the table for dinner and cake, and from there, people are going to be mingling and on the dance floor.

The thing about tab post-its is that they lose their stickiness easily and after a day or so will start to fall off, so as soon as you're finished putting together the poster board, write down each table number and the corresponding list of people who are sitting there so you can refer to that when creating your escort cards.

20:

THE WEEK OF YOUR WEDDING

The nice thing about having to be paid up with all vendors two weeks in advance is that the week of the wedding there is not much left to do but let it all happen. This is the time to get a manicure and pedicure (you MUST get shellac polish; it's chip resistant for a minimum of two weeks so it'll get you through your honeymoon, and it dries instantly, so no worries about smudges), get a facial, get a massage, and generally try not to spaz out.

This is also the time you'll have your final dress fitting. The day of my last fitting was very emotionally taxing for me for some reason. I just laid in bed and cried when I woke up. For some reason I kept thinking about all of the things that had upset me. I felt totally fine the next day…maybe I just needed to have a meltdown and get it over with. Or maybe it was the Blood Moon. Emotions are running high when you get so close to the wedding, so allow yourself to cry if you need to. (Just not the day before. No time for puffiness.)

During the last weeks leading up to the wedding, I began suffering from a "Wedding Brain" ailment. It's like Pregnancy Brain but there is no physical reason for it…it's strictly psychological. You could tell me something and three seconds later I forgot we even had the conversation. If it's feasible, take a few days off from work before the wedding. You won't get anything done.

The Day Before

Your dress rehearsal will most likely take place the day before your wedding. Bring your items for set up (guest book, candles, card box, etc) to give to the site coordinator so you don't have to worry about it the day of the wedding.

Your officiant should be at the dress rehearsal to give you a rundown of which way you'll come in so no one sees your dress, and it gives your bridal party practice so they remember the order that they walk in. Run through it at least three times so you have it down pat and there's no questions the day of, and be sure to include your ushers so they know how you want people being seated. If you're having someone read at the ceremony, you'll want to invite them too so that they know exactly where to go.

Here's the processional order at most weddings:

Bride's Mom (her entrance indicates that the ceremony is starting)

Groomsmen

Best Man

Groom (he can choose to walk alone or have his mother escort him)

Officiant

Bridesmaids

Maid /Matron of Honor

The Flower Girl and Ring Bearer (if there are any)

The Father of the Bride and the Bride (If your father has passed or you don't have the kind of relationship where you'd want him to walk you down the aisle, you can choose anyone else you'd like to escort you, or you can walk alone. The bride should be on the escort's left arm.)

Some grooms choose not to walk the aisle, and will enter from a side or back door with the officiant and best man and stand at the altar, watching everyone as they walk down the aisle.

Your groomsmen will join arms with your bridesmaids one at a time on the way out of the ceremony, so choose the order in which they'll walk in the processional accordingly. You can also choose to have your bridesmaids escorted by your groomsmen in the processional, having them enter one couple at a time. If you choose to do this, just make sure your MOH and Best Man walk last so that they'll be standing next to you and your groom at the altar. (They'll need to be next to you so that your MOH can hold your bouquet during the ceremony and both she and the Best Man can hold your rings.)

Jewish weddings have a different order. In a Jewish ceremony, the processional is as follows:

Rabbi and/or Cantor

Grandparents of the bride

Grandparents of the groom

Groomsmen, in pairs

Best man

Groom, escorted by both parents (father on his right, mother on his left)

Bridesmaids, single file or in pairs

Maid/matron of honor

Ring bearer and/or flower girl

The bride, escorted by both parents (father on her right, mother on her left)

If you don't care about tradition and you have a specific way you want people to walk in, don't sweat it- do it how you want to do it.

The dress rehearsal is so much fun. There's nervous energy because you're literally doing a walk-through of your wedding day and then after you get to let loose and have a good meal and good drinks with good friends. Do not overdo the drinks...the last thing you want is to be dehydrated and hung over for your wedding.

You'll need to make a reservation for your rehearsal dinner well in advance since it will likely be a large party. Check for any minimums for food and beverage before booking. It was much harder than I thought it would be to find a place that could accommodate our party size without a $1,000+ minimum! Delegate this task to someone else so you can cross it off of your "To Do" list. Etiquette dictates that you should send invitations for the rehearsal dinner, but I think that's an unnecessary expense for such a small party where you can simply email the details.

You may have heard that you should invite out-of-town guests to your rehearsal dinner, but that's not true; only invite them if you want them there. Your guest list for the dinner should include your parents, your wedding party and their spouses, ushers, and ceremony readers. If you want to invite grandparents, you can do that too. You've also probably heard that you should make "welcome baskets" to leave for out-of-town guests at their hotel rooms. While this is a very nice and thoughtful gesture, this also is not required. It's just one more thing to worry about.

Traditionally, the rehearsal dinner is paid for by the groom's parents, but be sure to check with them in advance.

The rehearsal dinner is the time when you and/or your fiancé should give a short speech about how much you appreciate your family and bridal party's support and hard work and how excited you are to celebrate with them.

I got exactly one hour of sleep the night before my wedding and I felt terrible. Do whatever you can to get a good night's sleep so you're fresh for your wedding day.

Wedding Day Packing List

Don't rely on memory...you'll be sure to forget something. Here's a sample list of what you need to bring with you the day of the ceremony:

- Marriage certificate (and pens to sign it with)
- Wedding Dress in garment bag
- Customized Hanger
- Veil/Headband/Tiara/Hair pin
- Wedding Shoes
- Vows
- Toss Garter and Keep Garter
- Comfortable shoes for dancing
- Earrings, necklace, bracelet
- Groom's wedding ring
- Groom's gift
- Ring bearer box or pillow
- Flower girl basket
- Petticoat/Hoop Skirt/Slip
- Strapless bra
- Undergarments
- Phone & Charger
- Makeup
- Wallet
- Clutch (to have on hand at the reception)
- Overnight bag
- Emergency Kit
- Tip Envelopes
- Invitation (for professional photos)
- Something old, new, borrowed & blue

Groom's Packing List

- Tuxedo in garment bag
- Tie
- Pocket square

- Dress socks
- Dress shoes
- Cuff links
- Watch
- Vows
- Hair gel
- Bride's wedding ring
- Bride's gift
- Phone & charger
- Overnight bag

The Day Of

You and your wedding party will have to adhere to a strict schedule when it comes to the day of your wedding. It's crucial to outline the day's events and give all wedding party members and immediate family a copy so everyone is on the same page about when they should be arriving and what to expect. Here's a sample wedding day guideline.

Wedding Day Timeline

9:00AM: Bride, bridesmaids & MOB arrive at hair & makeup salon

12:00PM: Groom arrives at venue & checks into hotel

2:30PM: Bride, Bridesmaids & groomsmen arrive at venue to check into hotel rooms

2:50PM: Groomsmen meet in best man's room, bridesmaids & MOB meet in bride's room

3:00PM: Photographer arrives for pre-wedding photos

4:00PM: Ushers arrive; MOG meets with groom for photos

4:30PM: Ushers begin seating guests. FOB meets in bride's room. MOG distributes boutonnieres.

4:50PM: Groom & groomsmen leave hotel room for ceremony

4:55 PM: Bride, FOB & bridesmaids leave hotel room for ceremony

5:00pm: Ceremony commences

5:30PM: Ceremony ends & cocktail hour begins. Formal family photos (parents, siblings, grandparents) at ceremony site

5:40PM: Transportation picks up bride, wedding party and photographer for photos offsite

7:00pm: Reception begins

7:05PM: Bridal party is introduced

7:15PM: Cake cutting, toasts

7:30PM: Dinner is served

The Speeches

It's completely up to you who makes a toast at your reception. Normally the Maid of Honor speaks, followed by the Best Man. You can also ask your parents if one of them are interested in speaking, especially if they're hosting. The bride and groom normally don't make a speech because it's kind of like you're toasting yourselves, but if you want to grab the mic for a second and thank everyone for coming and sharing this day with you two, that's perfectly fine.

What People Won't Tell You About the Wedding Day

Everyone tells you the wedding flies by...well GUESS WHAT? The actual time BEFORE the wedding DRAGS ON FOREVER. There's hair and makeup, checking into your hotel, signing the marriage certificate, individual wedding photos with your photographer, and in between, attempting to eat. (If you suffer from anxiety like I do, this will feel nearly impossible, but try to eat a little something; you don't want to pass out.)

Here's the deal: things are going to go wrong at your wedding. You may be thinking that you're so meticulously detail oriented that it's an impossibility, but you are wrong. The problem with weddings is that you can't control everyone else, and people make mistakes all the time. Hopefully for you it's something small, but somewhere, something is not going to go down the way it's supposed to. Here's a list of what went wrong for me:

Just as I was supposed to start taking photos of my mom zipping me into my dress, she yelled out that the hem on her dress had ripped. Thankfully my grandma had dropped off an emergency kit which included safety pins, so one of my bridesmaids helped her pin it back up.

When my coordinator came to tell us it was time to walk down the aisle I decided to go to the bathroom before leaving (I highly recommend you do this; nerves make you feel like you have to pee more often, and you don't want to be holding your legs together at the altar.) If you're wearing a ball gown, you will need someone's help. There is no getting around it. My mom helped me and as I leaned over I felt the back of my dress snap as the top clasp flew off. We safety pinned the back but it wouldn't stay, so my dress was loose in the chest all night.

I finally made it down the aisle, we said our vows, we kissed, and we were married. The actual ceremony is the part that goes by in a flash.

As we started receiving our plates at our reception I immediately got angry. The portions were about half of the size that they were in our food tasting and the food looked nothing like it did before. I told my MOH Rachelle not to eat hers as she is vegan and there was cheese on our eggplant dishes. It was made VERY clear on several occasions that this was to be a vegan meal (you know, the way we had it in our tastings..?). Rachelle flagged down the coordinator and told her that not only was there cheese on the eggplant but the entire dish was different. She gave some bullshit answer about how it was the same ingredients just "dressed up." Um, no. I was there for the tasting girlfriend. I hated the eggplant the day of the wedding but had loved it at the tasting. So, I didn't eat. They did bring out new dishes without cheese and gave us a refund on all of the eggplants for the mistake. If your food is not right, fight for a partial refund.

After I had carefully crafted our play list over many hours, my DJ decided he was only going to play *some* of our songs (and none of our slow songs.) Six very important, personal songs to my relationship with Joey did not get played. One of the only regrets I have from my wedding day is not saying anything to the DJ about playing strictly from our song list. If you're noticing that you're not into what's being played or they aren't playing enough songs from your list, speak up.

Though things will go awry at some point, you will end up married to the love of your life, and that's the most important part. I had quite a few things go wrong and I survived. It was frustrating, but those parts aren't what I think of when I think about the day.

Be sure to steal a few moments just for you and your new spouse throughout the night. One of the most common regrets from brides on their wedding day is that they wish they would have spent more time with their spouse, and I get it- it's tough to set aside the time when you have so many guests to speak to and so many things to do. When going around to all the tables to thank everyone for coming and to chat, go together. Remember, this is the day that you're celebrating your love and marriage, so be sure to make memories as a newly married couple at your wedding.

A wedding really shows how much the people who matter the most in your life really love you. Everyone in our wedding party did exactly what they were supposed to do and did it with a smile on their face. It really makes you take a step back and go, wow, these people are really amazing and I love them and they love me. (But it's still okay to be a little pissed about it not being perfect.)

The Day After

Give yourself a couple of buffer days before leaving for your honeymoon. The most tired I've ever been in my life was at the end of my wedding day. The day after the wedding should be spent lounging and reminiscing about all of the amazing times that were had the night before. I recommend a follow up brunch with your bridal party the day after the wedding so you can get all the details from them about what you missed from other guests (the stories are endless) and what a great time they had. For instance, I learned that one of my guests ate a pot cookie and started freaking out, and one of our ushers got so drunk that he puked all over the bathroom. Fun!

The day after is also a great time to open gifts. Just make sure you have a spreadsheet ready with who gave you what. I used our RSVP spreadsheet and added an additional column for gifts.

You'll notice that you didn't receive a gift from everyone. Guests technically have one year from the wedding date to give a gift (though, odds are if you don't get it that month, you aren't getting one at all.) You will inevitably get a couple of guests that don't give a gift. It's extremely rude and you'll want to say something, but just sock it into the memory bank and move on. You're supposed to send a thank you card to everyone who came to the wedding even if they didn't bring a gift, but I'm okay looking the other way if you decide against this.

21:

POST WEDDING

Just when you think you're finished, there's post-wedding tasks that you have to take care of. Don't worry, though. They're not nearly as emotionally taxing (or expensive.)

Changing Your Name

If you're changing your name, I know you're super excited to get it done, but save this until after the honeymoon. If your name on your license doesn't match your name on your passport and/or birth certificate, you're going to have a big problem.

The first thing you should do is change your name with the social security office. Call ahead of time to see if you can schedule an appointment. If you can't, get ready for a long wait. Check socialsecurity.gov to see which form you'll need to fill out for your state. Bring your certified birth certificate, your certified marriage license, and your social security card with you to the office. You'll get a new social security card with your new name (same number) mailed to you and you'll have to sign it with your new last name.

Next, get your name on your license changed. The social security office will give you proof in letter form that you've changed your name, and you should bring that with you along with your new card, your certified marriage certificate and birth certificate to either the

Secretary of State or DMV, depending on where you live. Check to see if your license will be expiring soon, and if it is, ask if you can just renew it then to get it all done at once since you have to take a picture for your new name anyway. My voter information was updated when I got a new license, but check with your secretary of state/DMV to see if you need to do anything else in your state.

Only after you receive your new license should you apply for a new passport. If you change your name within a year of obtaining your passport, you'll still need to send in proof of your name change, but there won't be a fee. You can get more details of passport name changes at travel.state.gov.

The next step is to change your name on your bank accounts. Some banks will give you a hard time without having your new ID, so if you can, wait until you get that, and bring your new social security card and marriage certificate as well. Ask for new debit cards with your new name.

Next up: employers, debtors and insurance. Your company won't know for sure if you've changed your name until you show them that you have. As for debtors, you'll likely have to fax proof of your new name with your marriage certificate to your mortgage company, utility companies, credit card companies, and car, home, and auto insurance companies. You'll also want to change your name at the post office to ensure that your bills get to your new name.

Basically, changing your name is a pain in the ass, and your significant other should be honored that you took the time.

Preserving Your Flowers

Simply put: ask your florist. They can tell you how to do it or do it for you for a fee. It's one of the things I regret not doing after my wedding as I would have liked to frame my bouquet. If you are planning on preserving your bouquet, make sure that you buy a smaller bouquet to toss so that you won't have to ask for it back from the person who catches it.

Preserving Your Dress

There are wedding gown preservationists that will clean your dress and preserve it in an archival box in acid-free paper so that your dress will stay in good shape without major yellowing and stains setting for years to come. This is especially important if you plan to pass down your dress.

Gowns can take a few to several weeks to be properly cleaned and preserved. Don't trust this to any dry cleaner; do some research on companies that specialize in bridal gown preservation, and ask your wedding salon who they trust to preserve gowns.

Some gown packages have a clear front so that you can see the dress wherever you store it. Be sure to store the gown out of light, which can wash it out.

Writing Your Thank You Cards

These will take a while, but suck it up. People took an entire day to spend with you to celebrate your wedding and then bought you a present, so a thank you note is a small token of appreciation. You have up to one year after the wedding to get them out, but a lot of people don't know this and think it's rude if they don't receive it within a few months. Trust me, you'll want to get them out of the way as soon as possible anyway so you don't have to worry about it anymore.

If you need some help thinking of what to say on your thank you cards, visit my TheRealistBride.com for some tips.

Review Your Vendors

You know how I told you 800 times to check reviews before booking each vendor? Now it's your turn to repay the favor to future brides. It's easier to write a review for bad experiences, but reward hard work and review the great experiences, too.

The Post-Wedding Blues

"I'll never be a bride again...now I'm just someone's wife."
-Monica Geller-Bing

Post-wedding depression is an actual ailment that some brides experience. It's not nearly as serious as actual depression, but after you've spent so much time and energy on one major event that's over in a day, it's normal to feel a little down when it's all said and done.

Take a look at your spouse. The real magic wasn't the event itself. It was that you took a day to commit to each other for life, and everyone meaningful to you shared in a celebration of your love. It's not about the wedding- it's about the *marriage*. Don't assume that the good stuff is over; the adventure is really just beginning.

22:

A FINAL WORD OF ADVICE

I just dumped a shitload of information on you, and it might seem overwhelming. It's okay to be overwhelmed, but it's not okay to try to take on everything by yourself. Ask for help from your family, your bridesmaids, and yes, your fiancé, wherever you can. If you try to do everything yourself, you're going to burn out.

Take everything one step at a time. Set up a calendar for yourself if it helps you and focus on one specific task that week to accomplish. Every time you get something done, give yourself a well deserved pat on the back. I know firsthand that planning a wedding isn't for sissies. Just as important: take breaks. You can't be all wedding all the time or you'll go insane. I know it feels like you'll never make it to the finish line, but you'll get there.

The good news: in my experience, the year after the wedding was much easier than the year before. Your stress level goes back to normal, your brain function goes back to normal, and your family goes back to normal (except now they're going to start asking you when you're having kids, if they haven't already.)

When you're planning your wedding, the most important piece of advice I can give you is to do what truly makes you happy. You're going to get tons of unsolicited advice, but that doesn't mean you have to take it. It's easy to lose sight of why you're getting married in the first place among family influence and constant wedding advertisements. Don't adhere to society or your family's expectations if it's not what you and your fiancé want. Your wedding is the perfect opportunity to let what makes you guys an amazing couple shine. You'll never regret being yourselves.

I wish you the best of luck with your wedding planning, a long and happy marriage, and that you don't kill anyone in the process.

-Jessica

Made in the USA
San Bernardino, CA
17 March 2019